# EVERY SEASON iS

# Soup
# Season

# EVERY SEASON IS

85+ Souper-Adaptable Recipes to Batch, Share, Reinvent, and Enjoy

Shelly Westerhausen Worcel
with Wyatt Worcel

## Soup Season

CHRONICLE BOOKS
SAN FRANCISCO

Library of Congress Cataloging-in-Publication Data available.

ISBN 978-1-7972-2030-7

Manufactured in China.

Prop and food styling by **Shelly Westerhausen Worcel**.
Design by **Lizzie Vaughan**.
Typeset in Dida, Faro, and Gooper.

10 9 8 7 6 5 4 3 2 1

Chronicle books and gifts are available at special quantity discounts to corporations, professional associations, literacy programs, and other organizations. For details and discount information, please contact our premiums department at corporatesales@chroniclebooks.com or at 1-800-759-0190.

Chronicle Books LLC
680 Second Street
San Francisco, California 94107
www.chroniclebooks.com

# CONTENTS

# SUMMER ☞ 166

# SOUP ENHANCERS ☞ 206

# ACCOMPANIMENTS ☞ 218

Caramelized Spring Onion Ramen  p. 141

# Introduction

Welcome to *Every Season Is Soup Season*! If you've already flipped through the pages before coming to read this introduction, you may find it odd that this is billed as a soup book when many of the recipes are for things besides soups. This is because it's a soup book and *also* a book about cooking once and enjoying twice—sometimes even three times! It's about celebrating the ease of creating a big pot of food and reinventing that soup the next day to create a completely new dish.

As I discovered when talking to people about writing this book, soup is very personal. Asked what their favorite soup is, people rarely give me the same response twice. I think this is because most people turn to soup for comfort, and comfort means so many different things to different people. It can mean craving vegetables or carbs or meat. It can mean wanting something hearty to fill you up, or light, to enjoy with a salad. Soup can be what you turn to when you are cooking to nourish just yourself or when hosting a huge dinner party. Some people think of soup when they want a quick weeknight meal and others when they are planning to spend all afternoon on a snowy day in the kitchen.

No one book can hope to meet everyone's ideal of soup, but I tried my best to incorporate as many different options as possible. There are light brothy soups, loaded hearty chilis, velvety cream soups, and chunky chowder options. All the soups are vegetarian, but many come with a meat option as well. The recipes can be made on the stovetop, and some include instructions for the slow cooker or pressure cooker. When developing these recipes, I also made sure to keep in mind that soup is meant to be flexible. Depending on your cooking style, you can follow a recipe to a T or use the recipe concept as inspiration and wander as far afield as you'd like.

Soups are a way to pack *way* more veggies into your family's dinner than they may even realize. Known for their economical properties, these one-pot wonders can feed a crowd (or yourself for several days). They can also act as a starting point for your next meal—dinner turned into the next day's breakfast or lunch and then some. I can't think of many dishes that are as versatile as a big pot of soup. I hope this book is just what you need to kick off your soup obsession.

# How to Use This Book

Maybe you loved the soup you made so much that you are going to eat it for the next three meals and be completely satisfied—that's great! Or maybe you tend to get bored with eating the same things twice, and as is the case for my husband, you won't eat leftovers unless they are masked as something new. This cookbook is all about choosing your own adventure. All you have to do is start with a soup recipe and go from there. You could (1) enjoy the soup on its own; (2) make it a meal with an Accompaniment (see pages 219 to 245), such as a salad or bread; and/or (3) whip up an array of toppings, or Soup Enhancers (see pages 207 to 217), to serve with the soup. Then, store the leftovers in the fridge to (1) reheat and enjoy as is the next day; (2) use the leftovers as a base for a new recipe (more on this on the next page!); or (3) freeze the leftover soup for a future rainy day. The choice is yours and I assure you there are no wrong answers!

The majority of the soups in this book are what I call everyday soups because they can be whipped up in under an hour. Personally, I lean toward soups that can be created and enjoyed on a weeknight without hours of simmering time. There are, of course, exceptions to this; long-simmered recipes like the French Onion Soup on page 107 are especially nice for when you are wanting to spend a few hours in the kitchen on a rainy Sunday.

## By Season

Because I've grown up with the rhythm of four seasons, I've fallen into a routine of making certain dishes during certain times of the year. I crave tomato soup and grilled cheese in the fall when the weather has started to cool but fresh, local tomatoes are still at their best. I love a hearty chili in the dead of winter after working up an appetite playing in the bitter cold. I can't resist a silky asparagus soup during the damp days of spring. As soon as the farmers pull up to the farmers' market with a pickup truck full of corn on the cob, I know I'll be making corn chowder.

This cookbook is organized by season, but as with most things in life, some of the recipes don't fit neatly into a single category. Some of the soups are clearly seasonal. For example, the Tomato-Watermelon Gazpacho on page 173 is best enjoyed when watermelons are at their growing peak and the muggy heat is settling into your skin. Some other recipes, like the Carrot-Orange-Ginger Soup on page 85, can be made in any season, as fresh carrots are available for a large portion of the year. Use the sections as a suggestion, but don't let that limit you. If you're craving Pumpkin & White Bean Soup (page 51) in the summertime, and you can get the ingredients, go for it!

### Meat Suggestions

I truly believe meals can be satisfying and delicious without meat, and all the soup recipes in this book are naturally vegetarian. It's how I cook and eat at home, as I've been a vegetarian for more than twenty-plus years. My husband, Wyatt, is not, and he often likes to make some sort of meat accompaniment to my vegetarian meals to satisfy his own cravings. So, in the same way we've done it in my previous two cookbooks, Wyatt will be hopping in here and there to offer meat suggestions in case you'd like to bulk up your meal with a little animal protein. I understand the conflict that can come from needing to satisfy many different dietary preferences, so I hope giving this extra option will be beneficial for some of you out there.

To make it as easy as possible to incorporate meat when desired, Wyatt perfected four easy meat accompaniment recipes—Mini Meatballs (page 217), Spicy Shrimp (page 216), Candied Bacon (page 216), and Shredded Chicken (page 217)—that easily fit into most of the soups in this book. Each soup recipe has a suggestion to let you know which meat accompaniment makes the most sense with that particular soup and how to incorporate it.

It's also worth noting that I often call for cheese in my recipes. If you are a vegetarian, make sure to use cheeses made without animal rennet. This comes up most often when it comes to hard cheeses such as Parmesan. Parmesan adds a wonderful salty flavor to soups, so vegetarian-friendly versions are worth seeking out at your local cheese shop or grocery store with an extensive cheese section.

# Repurposing Leftover Soup:
## Quick Fixes & New Twists

There are thirty-plus vegetarian base soup recipes in this book, and each recipe has one to three suggestions for dressing up or repurposing your leftover soup into new dishes. There are two kinds of repurposed "recipes" in this book:

 **Quick Fix**

These are small adjustments to bring new flavors to the soup you've got lingering in your fridge. Quick Fix suggestions include throwing in a handful of leafy greens, adding new toppings, incorporating additional spices, or serving with a grain to breathe new life into your already delicious soup recipe. All the Quick Fix options either allow you to prep things in advance or take only a few minutes to prepare on the spot (plus cooking time for some of the grain suggestions). Sometimes you just don't have the time or energy to create a whole new meal night after night, and in those situations, a Quick Fix can be your go-to.

 **New Twist**

These are completely new recipes you can make out of your leftover soup. For the most part, the New Twist recipes are entrées so you can use your leftover soup to make lunch or dinner the next day. Some require several cups of the soup (like the White Bean Hot Dish on page 156), while others require only a few tablespoons (see Tomato Butter on page 42 or Pumpkin Crème Fraîche Deviled Eggs on page 54). I've provided complete recipe instructions, so even beginner cooks can revamp their leftovers. For the cooks out there who might be using this book as a source for improvisation, you'll probably start to notice that some New Twist recipes can easily be translated from one recipe to another (for example, you could make tostadas with either the black bean soup on page 135 or the chili on page 155). Feel free to follow the New Twist recipes as they were written or get as creative as you'd like!

# A (Somewhat Quick– I Promise!) Equipment Guide

This section is not an exhaustive list of every single piece of equipment you need but rather a few must-haves to create an enjoyable and easy soup-cooking experience.

I utilize three different cooking methods for the soups in this book: stovetop, pressure cooking, and slow cooking. When it doesn't compromise flavor or texture, I will give you alternative instructions in the recipe in case you'd like to use a different method. The main recipe will always indicate my preferred way of cooking the soup. (For example, I love to use a pressure cooker to make the black bean soup on page 135 to speed up the process, so that's what the main recipe calls for.) Here is the equipment you'll need for each cooking method:

 **Dutch oven or large stockpot with lid**

For stovetop cooking, you'll want a large enameled Dutch oven or a stainless-steel stockpot. I find that my enameled Dutch oven retains heat well and is the easiest to clean, but a large stainless-steel stockpot will work just fine if it's what you have.

 **Pressure cooker**

I love to use an electric pressure cooker when I'm in a hurry and I want to develop flavor quickly without too much effort. I used a 6 qt [5.7 L] Instant Pot to test all the pressure-cooking recipes in this book. Not all pressure cookers work the same, so there may be some situations where I suggest you follow the instructions for your specific model.

 **Slow cooker**

This hands-off method is essential when I know I'm going to have a busy day and want to prep everything ahead of time, knowing dinner will be ready when I finish up work. Slow cookers tend to be pretty consistent in their settings; the recipes in this book mostly utilize the high and low settings.

Although not required for all soups in this book, the following equipment will come in handy for many recipes:

**Immersion blender**

I highly recommend this small piece of equipment if you are planning to make any of the puréed soups in this book. Although you could use a regular blender in a pinch, trying to dump hot soup into a blender and then blend it while leaving room for the steam to escape is a little bit like playing with fire, as it's easy to spill scorching soup on yourself. An immersion blender will allow you to blend the soup right in the pot.

**High-speed blender or food processor**

Many of the recipes in this book (including sauces, dips, cold soups, dough, etc.) require you to use either a blender or food processor to achieve a smooth consistency.

**Fine-mesh strainer**

I use this to rinse grains and strain liquids. It will come in handy particularly when making Homemade Roasted Vegetable Broth (page 209).

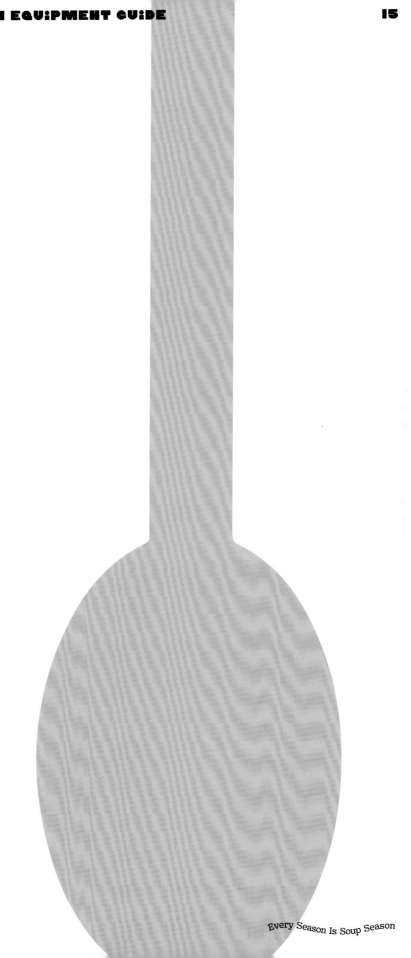

### Wooden spoon or heatproof silicone spoons

These are my utensils of choice when stirring spices and aromatics into my soups.

### Ladle

Having at least one large ladle on hand will make getting your soup from the cooking vessel to serving bowls a breeze. If you find yourself without one when it's time to serve, a large measuring cup will work.

### Instant-read thermometer

If you are making any of the bread recipes in this book, I highly suggest investing in an instant-read thermometer to make sure that your bread is at the correct temperature when you remove it from the oven. I also use this when reheating soup and leftovers to make sure they reach the recommended temperature of 165°F [75°C].

I also always have shallow serving bowls and soup spoons on hand, which I cover a bit more in the serving section (see page 22).

# A Flavor Guide

In addition to using a flavorful base and quality ingredients, the key to making an exceptional soup is balance. I love to play with textural balance by adding crunchy toppings to creamy soups—think chips, quick-pickled vegetables, and croutons. (Have you ever topped potato soup with potato chips? Definitely recommend—see Quick Fix, page 31.) Or by adding doughy dumplings to chunky stews (see Roasted Root Vegetable & Dumpling Soup on page 101). Adding a creamy sauce at the end (like the Green Tahini on page 212 or Cider-Mustard Glaze on page 211) can enhance more than just the flavor profile of your soup.

Although texture is pretty easy to adjust regardless of your experience level, learning to balance flavors can be more of a challenge. I've done my best to make every soup as vibrant as possible, but everyone's taste buds are different. Something that tastes perfect to me might be too salty or too acidic for you. I've used the same baseline amount of salt in all of my recipes so you'll know after making one soup recipe if you prefer more or less salt than I do and can adjust in the future. I know a lot of recipe writers these days are leaning toward telling everyone to use Diamond Crystal salt for consistency, but I'm going to complicate things by going against the grain here. Not only is Diamond Crystal not widely available in the Midwest, but they are owned by a company I don't feel comfortable backing. All the recipes in this book have been tested with Jacobsen Kosher Sea Salt and sometimes Morton's. This isn't to say you need to use these exact brands for these recipes. Use whatever salt you are used to, as you will most likely know how much feels right based on your experience cooking with it.

Although salt is what we use most often to season our food, play around with the following flavors and ingredients when seasoning your soups:

### Acid
Add vinegar (champagne, red wine, apple cider, etc.), wine, or citrus juice (usually lemon or lime) to taste at the very end of cooking

### Creamy
Dollop or stir in canned coconut milk, crème fraîche, sour cream, heavy cream, or whole milk

### Fat
Drizzle or stir in olive oil, brown butter, ghee, or flavored oils

### Herbs
Add dried herbs such as rosemary, oregano, or basil before cooking; top with or stir in sauces like pesto at the end; or garnish with fresh chopped herbs such as parsley, cilantro, or tarragon

### Salt/Umami
Salt options include sea salt, smoked salt, and flaky fleur de sel; for umami look to miso, tomato paste, soy or tamari sauce, grated Parmesan cheese, or Worcestershire sauce

### Spice
Harissa, hot sauce, chipotle in adobo sauce, chopped fresh chiles

Rice & Lentil Pilaf with Pickled Raisins & Pistachios  p.144

Sweet Potato & Leek Peanut Stew  p. 95

As you experiment to find the balance that is just right for you, you are bound to go too far from time to time. Although these solutions won't fix all problems, here are a few suggestions for how to adjust an out-of-balance soup:

### Too salty

This one should be an easy fix. If you've oversalted your soup or cooked it down for too long, simply add more water or low-sodium broth to dilute it. If you are worried about it becoming too watery, you could add dairy instead (heavy cream, sour cream, milk), or add a peeled raw potato or two and let the potato soak up the excess salt.

### Too spicy

Add some acid (lemon juice, vinegar) or dairy (milk, sour cream, or heavy cream) to tame the heat.

### Too acidic

Add broth or water, taste, and re-season to adjust any other flavors that may have become off-balance with the additional liquid.

### Too thin

There are a few options here, and the best solution will depend on what kind of soup you are making. If it's a chunky soup, cook the soup down to thicken it (although be careful not to make it too salty); scoop out a cup or so of the soup, purée it, and stir it back in; or add pasta or grains to absorb some of the liquid. If it's a puréed soup, thicken it by blending in cream, yogurt, white beans, cooked potato, or bread.

### Too thick

You'll need to add some additional liquid. Depending on the flavors of your soup, the best option could be broth, water, wine, beer, heavy cream, or milk.

Pressure Cooker Black Bean Soup with Orange & Cumin  p. 135

# Serving

One thing I love about soup is just how unfussy it can be; it's usually just as delicious eaten right away as it is reheated after a day or so. With that being said, here's what I've found to be the optimal way to serve hot soup. Let the soup sit off the burner for about 15 minutes to develop flavor. It will still be plenty warm if you keep it covered in a Dutch oven, or you can reheat it gently on the stove if it gets cooler than you like. When you're ready to serve, heat the soup bowls in a 200°F [95°C] oven for 5 minutes. Then ladle the soup into the warm bowls, garnish, and enjoy!

Depending on the recipe, soup makes a wonderful starter, entrée, and even dessert. When serving it as a starter or dessert, use smaller bowls, about half the size of a salad plate. When serving as a main entrée, use big shallow bowls, which leave lots of surface area for toppings. I always serve my soups with soup spoons, since they tend to be wider and scoop up soup more easily.

As you'll discover when flipping through this book, I don't shy away from garnishes. I find that they bring extra interest, and the presentation can really wow guests. If your soup is creamy, drizzle or swirl in vibrant sauces such as Green Tahini (page 212), thinned-out yogurt or sour cream, a jazzed-up oil (such as Tarragon-Orange Oil on page 210), or a nice olive oil. To bring texture and visual interest, top with a mound of croutons (page 215), Frizzled Shallots (page 211), chunks of cheese (such as Honeyed Feta with Black & White Sesame Seeds on page 214), and/or handfuls of chopped herbs. If you plan to let family and guests serve themselves, place small bowls filled with garnish options and small spoons near the serving area so guests can drizzle, scoop, and sprinkle the toppings into their bowls as desired.

## Serving Size

I've found that setting serving sizes for soups is more difficult than for other recipes I've developed. Some soups are more filling than others based on what ingredients are in them, so I've kept that in mind. Bulking up the soup with a meat addition will alter the serving size as well. Use my serving sizes as a general guide (usually around 1½ cups [360 ml] for chunky soups and 2 cups [480 ml] per serving for creamy soups), but also keep in mind the context and the people you are serving. Are you feeding hungry teens after soccer practice? A group of friends for a quick summer lunch with salad and bread? A hearty winter dinner after a full day of skiing? All the savory soup recipes in this book are portioned to be served as the main component of the meal along with a side salad or bread. If serving the soup as an appetizer or side, you'll probably get more portions out of each batch.

The soups in this book are easy to scale up as needed. They can be doubled or even tripled if you have a large-enough pot to cook them in. Although you could potentially scale these recipes down, I don't recommend it, as you may not end up with enough liquid to actually simmer your ingredients in. Instead, I recommend making the recipe as written and using some of my suggestions for leftovers to use up any extra.

Tomato Watermelon Gazpacho p. 173

Summer Garden Minestrone p. 181

Pumpkin & White Bean Soup with Brown Butter Sage  P. 51

# Storing & Freezing Soup

How best to store a soup depends on what is in it, so I've provided specific storing information within each recipe. With that being said, there are a few general notes that apply to most situations.

One universal rule: Pasta or grains in a soup will get mushy over time, so it's best to cook and store the pasta or grains separately. This will require a bit of planning when you go to make your soup, as you'll have to ask yourself if you want to take the easy route of cooking it all together to enjoy right away or cook the grains or pasta separately for better leftovers. If you cook them together and have leftovers, the soup will still be edible if stored properly in the fridge, but its texture won't hold up and will require adding more liquid when reheating.

## In the Fridge

You should always let soup cool down slightly before putting it in the fridge, but make sure the soup doesn't sit out for more than 2 hours. The easiest way to do this is to leave it on the turned-off stove while you eat. If you are short on time, you can quickly cool down a soup by placing the pot in a bath of ice water. Once it's no longer piping hot, transfer the soup to an airtight container, cover, and refrigerate. Most soups will keep in the fridge for about 3 days.

To reheat, transfer the soup to a pot. Cook over medium heat until it reaches at least 165°F [75°C]. There is a good chance your soup will have thickened up in the fridge, so you may need to stir in broth or water to thin it out.

## In the Freezer

My goal in this book is to provide you with such mouthwatering left-over ideas that you don't end up with any soup to freeze. However, if the rare occasion does come up, this section should be useful.

Before we jump into the how, I do need to warn you that not all soups freeze well. Here are a few ingredients that don't hold up well in your soup in the freezer:

| Dairy products (milk, cream, cheese) may separate in the freezer. | Pasta, rice, and potatoes tend to get mushy when frozen. | Any fresh herbs or garnishes that your recipe calls for adding at the end should not be frozen with the soup. |

But fear not—this doesn't mean you can't freeze soups with these ingredients, but I do suggest you do a little planning ahead of time. If you plan to freeze some of your soup, remove the portion you are freezing before adding these ingredients, and make a note on the container that these items need to be added when it is reheated.

Now that you've sorted out whether your soup is freezer-worthy, here are my tips and suggestions on the best way to freeze:

 **Cool it**

As with fridge storage, you'll want to let the soup cool first before putting it in the freezer. To speed up the process, you can put the pot containing the soup in a bath of ice water and stir the soup every few minutes.

 **Containers**

Use a freezer-safe container, such as tempered glass with a sealable lid, BPA-free plastic, or a freezer-friendly zip-top bag, that will fit the portion size you'll need for your next meal. Leave about 1 in [2.5 cm] of space between the soup and the top of the container to give the soup room to expand, but don't allow so much space that excess air could lead to freezer burn. I prefer reusable containers, but if you are short on freezer space, zip-top bags can be frozen flat so they are easily stackable (do not stack until the bags are frozen).

 **Label it**

Most soups will stay good for about 3 months in the freezer. Make sure to properly label your soup, noting what it is, any special reheating instructions, any garnishes that will need to be prepped at the time of reheating, and the use-by date.

 **Reheat**

To reheat, thaw in the fridge overnight or, if short on time, place the container in a warm water bath until mostly thawed. Transfer to a pot and heat over medium heat to at least 165°F [75°C]. If your soup is too thick, add broth or water to thin it out. And don't forget to prepare some garnish options (lemon wedges, fresh herbs, etc.) to refresh the soup before serving.

Smoky French Lentil Soup with White Balsamic Reduction  p.143

# Gruyère, Cauliflower & Potato Soup

Serves 4

2 Tbsp olive oil

1 yellow onion, chopped

3 garlic cloves, minced

1 tsp fresh thyme leaves

½ Tbsp salt

1 tsp freshly ground black pepper

1 large cauliflower (about 2 lb [910 g]), cored and cut into 1 in [2.5 cm] pieces

1 lb [455 g] Yukon gold potatoes, peeled and cut into 1 in [2.5 cm] pieces

4 cups [960 ml] Homemade Roasted Vegetable Broth (page 209) or store-bought low-sodium vegetable broth

5¼ oz [150 g] Gruyère cheese, shredded

1 tsp fresh lemon juice

4 tsp Pickled Mustard Seeds (page 213; optional)

## Meat Suggestion

Top with crumbled Candied Bacon (page 216) when serving.

### Quick Fix

Swap out the Pickled Mustard Seeds for Fennel-Rye Croutons (page 215) or top with sour cream (crème fraîche if you're feeling fancy), minced fresh dill, and crushed potato chips.

I can't think of a soup more comforting than a velvety potato and cheese soup. This one hits just right. The cauliflower lightens it up, and the pickled mustard seeds add acid and pop that make you want to go back again and again for another bite.

1. In a large stockpot or Dutch oven over medium-low heat, warm the oil. Add the onion and sauté until soft and translucent, 5 to 7 minutes. Add the garlic, thyme, 1 tsp of the salt, and the pepper and sauté until fragrant, 30 seconds.

2. Add the cauliflower, potatoes, vegetable broth, and 2 cups [480 ml] of water. Bring to a boil over high heat. Lower the heat to medium-low and simmer until the potatoes and cauliflower are tender and easily pierced with a fork, 12 to 15 minutes.

3. Remove from the heat and use an immersion blender to blend until smooth or (carefully!) purée in a blender in batches. Return the soup to the pot and stir in the Gruyère. Cook over medium-low heat, stirring, until the cheese is completely melted, about 3 minutes.

4. Remove from the heat. Stir in the lemon juice and remaining ½ tsp of salt. Taste and add salt, pepper, and lemon juice as needed. Divide between four bowls and sprinkle 1 tsp of pickled mustard seeds, if desired, into each bowl. Serve right away.

☞ **Pressure Cooker:** Use the sauté function to cook the onion, garlic, thyme, salt, and pepper in the pot of your pressure cooker as described in step 1 (alternatively, if your pressure cooker doesn't have a sauté function, do this step on the stovetop, then pour the mixture into your pressure cooker). Add the cauliflower, potatoes, vegetable broth, and 1½ cups [360 ml] of water. Cover and seal, making sure the venting valve is closed. Pressure cook on high for 5 minutes, then quick release. Continue as directed in the recipe from step 3.

☞ **Storing:** Store leftovers refrigerated in an airtight container for up to 3 days or freeze for up to 2 months.

# Gruyère-Cauliflower-Potato Gravy over 7-Minute Eggs & Biscuits

**Serves 2**

4 eggs

1 cup [240 ml] Gruyère,
Cauliflower & Potato Soup
(page 31)

½ tsp tamari or soy sauce

¼ tsp Dijon mustard

4 homemade or store-bought
biscuits

1 Tbsp chopped fresh chives

Salt

Freshly crushed black pepper

Hot sauce, for serving

Potatoes and eggs are a classic combo, so I decided a potato gravy would be delicious for breakfast. Wyatt is a biscuits-and-gravy snob, so when he saw me turning this soup into a "gravy" he was appalled. He not-so-politely reminded me that just because something looks like gravy does not mean it will taste like gravy. And he's technically right: This isn't a traditional gravy of the sort that uses meat drippings and is thickened with flour. But I was also right! By adding a little tamari for umami and lots of crushed black pepper, this soup's creaminess and savoriness turns a pile of eggs and biscuits into the perfect breakfast-for-dinner or lazy brunch. Wyatt cleaned his plate when I served him this, by the way.

1. Fill a medium saucepan with water and bring to a boil over high heat. Use a spoon to carefully lower the eggs into the water. Lower the heat to medium-low and simmer for 7 minutes.

2. Drain and run the eggs under cold water until they are cool enough to handle, about 1 minute. Peel the eggs and quarter them.

3. Meanwhile, bring the soup to a simmer in a small saucepan over medium heat. Stir in the tamari and mustard. Keep warm over low heat.

4. To serve, split the biscuits in half and divide them between two plates. Top with the eggs, drizzle with potato "gravy," and sprinkle chives, salt, pepper, and a few drops of hot sauce over it all. Serve right away.

# Roasted Tomato Soup

Serves 6

3 lb [1.4 kg] plum tomatoes, halved

2 small or 1 medium shallot, quartered

4 garlic cloves, crushed

6 thyme sprigs

¼ cup [60 ml] olive oil

½ tsp red pepper flakes

2 tsp salt

½ tsp freshly ground black pepper

One 28 oz [800 g] can whole tomatoes

2 cups [480 ml] Homemade Roasted Vegetable Broth (page 209) or store-bought low-sodium vegetable broth

1 Tbsp tomato paste

1 Tbsp unsalted butter

½ tsp dried oregano

1 Tbsp red wine vinegar

1 Tbsp sugar (optional)

Smoked Gouda Grilled Cheese Croutons (page 215) and chopped fresh basil, for serving (optional)

**Meat Suggestion**

Candied Bacon (page 216) can be crumbled over the soup.

**Quick Fix**

Turn your leftover soup into a comforting pasta meal with the addition of cheese tortellini and spinach. Bring a large stockpot of salted water to a boil. Add one 9 oz [255 g] package of tortellini and cook according to the package directions. Meanwhile, warm up 4 cups [960 ml] of leftover Roasted Tomato Soup in a medium saucepan. Drain the tortellini and add it to the soup along with 1 cup [20 g] fresh baby spinach. Cook, stirring constantly, until the spinach wilts, about 1 minute, top with torn fresh basil, and serve right away.

I love to make this soup in early fall when the weather has just started to cool off and the last of the tomatoes are still lingering at the farmers' market. To make sure the star ingredient really shines through, I use freshly roasted tomatoes, canned tomatoes, *and* tomato paste. Although this soup is delicious on its own, the Smoked Gouda Grilled Cheese Croutons (page 215) will take it over the top. Make a batch while the tomatoes are roasting and serve them on top. You may not need a full tablespoon of sugar if your tomatoes are sweet, so start by adding just a little bit, taste, and add more as needed.

**1.** Preheat the oven to 400°F [200°C]. In a 9 by 13 in [23 by 33 cm] baking dish, add the fresh tomatoes, shallots, garlic, and thyme and toss with the oil. Spread into an even layer and sprinkle with the red pepper flakes, ½ tsp of the salt, and the black pepper. Roast until starting to fall apart, about 45 minutes. Scoop out the thyme sprigs with a fork.

**2.** Transfer the tomato mixture to a large stockpot and add the canned tomatoes with their juice, vegetable broth, tomato paste, butter, oregano, and ½ tsp of the salt. Bring to a boil over high heat. Lower the heat to medium-low and simmer for 10 minutes so the flavors can meld and develop.

**3.** Remove from the heat and stir in the vinegar and the remaining 1 tsp salt. Use an immersion blender to blend to the desired consistency. Taste and add sugar if needed. Season with salt, pepper, and vinegar as needed. Serve warm, topped with the croutons and basil, if desired.

☞ **Slow Cooker:** Roast the tomatoes following the instructions in step 1. Transfer to a slow cooker and add the canned tomatoes with their juice, 1½ cups [360 ml] of vegetable broth (instead of 2 cups [480 ml]), tomato paste, butter, oregano, and ½ tsp salt. Cook on high for 2 hours. Finish the soup as described in step 3.

☞ **Storing:** Store leftovers refrigerated in an airtight container for up to 3 days or freeze for up to 2 months.

# Ricotta Gnocchi with Vodka Sauce

**Serves 4**

One 15 oz [430 g] container
whole-milk ricotta

2 eggs

3 oz [85 g] Parmesan cheese,
grated (about 3 cups), plus more
for serving

½ tsp salt

¼ tsp freshly ground
black pepper

¾ to 1 cup [105 to 140 g]
all-purpose flour

1 Tbsp unsalted butter

¼ cup [55 g] tomato paste

1½ cups [360 ml] Roasted
Tomato Soup (page 37)

1 cup [240 ml] heavy cream

¼ cup [60 ml] vodka

Red pepper flakes,
for serving (optional)

Did you miss the dairy in my Roasted Tomato Soup (page 37) recipe? Don't fret: This vodka sauce makes up for it with plenty of heavy cream. Don't skip the step of draining the ricotta, or your gnocchi will be too wet and likely to fall apart when boiling. If you are short on time, feel free to use store-bought gnocchi. This dish will still be delicious and perfect for an easy weeknight meal.

1. Transfer the ricotta to a fine-mesh strainer set over a large bowl. Place in the fridge to drain for at least 30 minutes. Line a baking sheet with parchment paper and set aside.

2. In a large bowl, whisk the eggs. Add the drained ricotta, 1 oz [30 g] of the Parmesan (about 1 cup), the salt, and pepper and mix until combined. Add ¾ cup [105 g] of flour and mix to create a sticky dough, adding more flour, a little at a time, if needed until the dough holds its shape, up to 1 cup [140 g] total. Set aside.

3. In a saucepan over medium heat, melt the butter. Add the tomato paste and cook until fragrant, about 3 minutes, stirring often. Add the soup and simmer for 5 minutes, then stir in the heavy cream. Remove from the heat.

4. Meanwhile, bring a large pot of salted water to a boil over high heat. Drop about twelve Tbsp-size pieces of the gnocchi dough into the water. My favorite way to do this is to scoop the dough using a spoon and then use another spoon to scrape the dough into the pot. Boil until the gnocchi start to float, about 3 minutes. Use a slotted spoon to transfer the gnocchi to the prepared baking sheet. Repeat with the remaining dough.

5. When you are cooking your last batch of gnocchi, put the sauce back over medium heat. Add the vodka and ½ cup [120 ml] of gnocchi cooking water and bring to a simmer. Stir in the remaining 2 oz [55 g] of Parmesan (about 2 cups) and cook until the cheese is melted and incorporated, 1 minute more.

6. Divide the gnocchi among four bowls and top with the sauce. Top each bowl with a sprinkle of grated Parmesan and red pepper flakes, if desired. Serve right away.

# Tomato Butter

**Makes 1¼ cup [300 g]**

1 cup [220 g] unsalted butter,
at room temperature

⅔ cup [160 ml] Roasted
Tomato Soup (page 37)

Don't have enough Roasted Tomato Soup (page 37) left over for a full meal? Make this tomato compound butter. It's delicious slathered on toast with a fried or hard-boiled egg. Wyatt also suggests you use it on your BLT to bring in an extra punch of tomato flavor. You are working quite a bit of liquid into fat, so at first the butter will look like it won't come together, but keep blending, and eventually it will create a pink and creamy spread.

**1.** Add the butter and soup to a food processor fitted with a blade attachment. Pulse a few times to break up the butter. Purée, stopping to scrape down the sides often, until the tomato soup has fully incorporated into the butter, about 3 minutes. Serve right away or store in an airtight container in the fridge for up to 3 days.

# White Bean Stew with Marinated Radicchio

**Serves 4 to 6**

### Marinated Radicchio

1 small head radicchio, cored and leaves torn into 2 in [5 cm] pieces

Grated zest and juice (about 3 Tbsp) of 1 lemon

1 Tbsp olive oil

¼ tsp salt

### Soup

¼ cup [60 ml] olive oil

1 small fennel bulb, trimmed, cored, and thinly sliced

1 yellow onion, finely chopped

6 garlic cloves, minced

1 tsp fresh thyme

½ tsp red pepper flakes

1 tsp salt

¼ cup [60 ml] dry white wine

Two 15½ oz [445 g] cans white beans, such as cannellini or great Northern, rinsed

4 cups [960 ml] Homemade Roasted Vegetable Broth (page 209) or store-bought low-sodium vegetable broth

¼ tsp freshly ground black pepper

1 Tbsp fresh lemon juice

¼ cup [3 g] chopped fresh dill

Grated Parmesan cheese, for serving

### Meat Suggestion

Stir in a few Mini Meatballs (page 217) at the end of cooking, right before adding the marinated radicchio.

### Quick Fix

Swirl in a drizzle of Tarragon-Orange Oil (page 210) after reheating the soup.

This hearty bean stew is livened up by the slightly bitter tang of marinated radicchio, which gets added at the end so it keeps a bit of crunch. Massaging the radicchio and letting it marinate cuts down on its bitterness (make sure you marinate only as much radicchio as you'll eat right away). If you aren't a fan of bitter greens, you can swap in Lacinato kale here.

Store the soup without the radicchio so it doesn't get soggy (and so you can make White Bean & Dill Dip [page 48] the next day!).

**1.** **Make the marinated radicchio:** In a medium bowl, combine the radicchio, lemon zest and juice, oil, and salt. Using clean hands, massage the radicchio for a few minutes or until it's completely coated and slightly softened. Set aside to marinate at room temperature for at least 30 minutes.

**2.** **Meanwhile, make the soup:** In a Dutch oven or large stockpot over medium heat, warm the oil. Add the fennel and onion and sauté until softened, 5 to 7 minutes. Add the garlic, thyme, red pepper flakes, and salt and sauté until fragrant, 30 seconds. Add the wine and simmer until the wine is mostly cooked off, 2 to 3 minutes. Add the beans, vegetable broth, and pepper, raise the heat to high, and bring to a boil. Lower the heat to medium-low and simmer for 15 minutes.

**3.** Remove from the heat and stir in the lemon juice and the dill. Taste and season with salt, pepper, and lemon juice as needed. Divide the soup between four to six bowls and top with marinated radicchio and Parmesan. Serve warm.

☞ **Pressure Cooker:** Prepare the marinated radicchio as instructed in step 1. Starting at step 2, use the sauté option on your pressure cooker to sauté the aromatics and reduce the wine. Add 3½ cups [840 ml] of vegetable broth instead of 4 cups [960 ml]. Pressure cook on high for 5 minutes (making sure the pressure valved is closed), quick release the pressure, and remove the lid. Proceed with step 3.

☞ **Storing:** Store the radicchio and soup refrigerated in separate airtight containers for up to 3 days. The soup (not the radicchio) should also be OK in the freezer for up to 2 months, but the beans will lose most of their texture, so I do not recommend it.

# White Bean & Dill Dip

**Serves 6 to 8 as a snack**

2 cups [480 ml] White Bean
Stew (page 47)

⅔ cup [160 g] sour cream

4 oz [115 g] cream cheese

⅓ cup [4 g] packed fresh dill,
plus more for serving

1 tsp champagne vinegar
or rice vinegar

¼ tsp salt

2 Tbsp olive oil,
plus more for serving

Freshly ground black pepper

Purée leftover soup into a velvety-smooth green dip that is perfect for snacking. Serve it with crackers, chips, or raw veggies as an appetizer or a quick bite. Or, spread it on thick slices of bread, top with roasted veggies or marinated radicchio, and pair with a side salad to make a complete meal. Don't skip the draining step; it's always much easier to add a little extra water if it's too thick than to save it from being too thin!

**1.** Put the stew in a colander in the sink and rinse it a bit with water. Shake the colander to remove excess water and drain for 5 minutes.

**2.** Transfer to a food processor and add the sour cream, cream cheese, dill, vinegar, and salt. Turn on the food processor and slowly pour in the oil. Process until smooth and velvety, about 30 seconds.

**3.** Transfer the dip to a serving bowl. Drizzle with a little more oil and sprinkle with pepper and more dill. Serve right away or store in an airtight container in the fridge for up to 2 days.

# Pumpkin & White Bean Soup with Brown Butter Sage

Serves 4 to 6 as a main
or 16 as a starter

### Soup

2 Tbsp unsalted butter

2 white onions, diced

1 Tbsp fresh rosemary,
or 2 tsp dried

2 garlic cloves, minced

1 tsp curry powder

½ Tbsp salt

½ tsp freshly ground
black pepper

¼ tsp grated nutmeg

Pinch of ground cloves

2 Tbsp maple syrup

⅓ cup [80 ml] apple cider

4 cups [960 ml] Homemade
Roasted Vegetable Broth
(page 209) or store-bought low-
sodium vegetable broth

Two 15½ oz [445 g] cans white
beans, such as cannellini or
great Northern, rinsed

Two 15 oz [430 g] cans
pumpkin purée

### Brown Butter Sage

2 Tbsp unsalted butter

12 fresh sage leaves,
rinsed and patted dry

### Meat Suggestion

Crumble Candied Bacon
(page 216) over the finished soup
instead of—or in addition to—the
Brown Butter Sage for an extra
boost of sweet and savory.

### Quick Fix

Make a batch of Pickled Mustard
Seeds (page 213) or Cider-Mustard
Glaze (page 211) to use as a topping
instead of the brown butter sage.

I had only planned to include one pumpkin soup recipe in this book, but after testing this one and the Coconut Pumpkin Curry Red Lentil Stew (page 59) side by side, I couldn't choose a favorite. Aside from its irresistible fall flavors, there are a couple of things that make this soup so special. First up, it uses canned pumpkin, which cuts down on the prep. Second, the white beans add creaminess and protein without altering the flavor too much. This soup is delicious on a cool fall or winter night served as a meal with some crusty bread or as a soup shooter at your holiday gathering.

1. **Make the soup:** In a large Dutch oven or stockpot over medium heat, melt the butter. Add the onions and cook until very soft and translucent, 10 to 12 minutes. Add the rosemary, garlic, curry powder, salt, pepper, nutmeg, and cloves and sauté until fragrant, another 30 seconds. Add the maple syrup and cook until mostly absorbed, 3 to 5 minutes. Add the cider and cook, stirring often, until reduced by half, 2 to 3 minutes.

2. Add the vegetable broth, beans, and pumpkin and bring to a boil over high heat. Lower the heat to medium-low and simmer for 15 minutes to develop the flavor. Remove from the heat and use an immersion blender to blend until smooth. Let cool enough to taste and season with salt and pepper.

3. **Meanwhile, make the brown butter sage:** In a small skillet over medium heat, melt the butter. Let the butter sizzle, swirling the pan around, until it is golden brown and nutty smelling. Remove from the heat and add the sage leaves (being careful that they are dry, as they may splatter the butter if wet.) Toss the sage in the butter to coat.

4. Divide the soup among serving bowls or small glasses and top each with a spoonful of brown butter and the sage.

☞ **Pressure Cooker:** Use the sauté function on the pressure cooker to do step 1. Stir in the vegetable broth, beans, and pumpkin. Pressure cook on high for 6 minutes, then do a quick release. Use an immersion blender to blend the soup until smooth, season with salt and pepper, and continue with the recipe at step 3.

☞ **Storing:** Store leftovers refrigerated in an airtight container for up to 4 days or freeze for up to 2 months.

# Stovetop Pumpkin Mac & Cheese with Roasted Brussels Sprouts

**Serves 8**

1 lb [455 g] Brussels sprouts, trimmed and halved

2 Tbsp olive oil

½ tsp salt

¼ tsp freshly ground black pepper

1 lb [455 g] elbow macaroni

4 Tbsp [55 g] unsalted butter

¼ cup [35 g] all-purpose flour

2 cups [480 ml] whole milk

1 cup [240 ml] Pumpkin & White Bean Soup (page 51)

1 tsp ground mustard

¼ tsp cayenne pepper

Pinch of grated nutmeg

8 oz [230 g] Cheddar cheese, shredded

2 oz [55 g] Parmesan cheese, grated

Chopped fresh chives, for serving

This extra-cheesy stovetop-pasta dish is familiar enough to please the whole family while still being packed with more veggies (pumpkin! Brussels sprouts!) than traditional mac and cheese. Serve this with one of the salads on pages 221 to 231 to complete the meal.

**1.** Preheat the oven to 400°F [200°C] and line a baking sheet with parchment paper. Toss the Brussels sprouts on the sheet with the oil, salt, and pepper, then spread out in a single layer. Roast for 20 to 25 minutes, tossing halfway through, or until tender and starting to brown in spots. Set aside.

**2.** Meanwhile, bring a large pot of salted water to a boil. Add the macaroni and cook according to the package directions. Drain and set aside.

**3.** In a large Dutch oven or stockpot over medium heat, melt the butter. Whisk in the flour and then slowly whisk in the milk. Simmer, whisking often, until the sauce is thick and coats the back of a spoon, 3 to 4 minutes. Lower the heat to medium-low and stir in the soup, mustard, cayenne, and nutmeg. Continue to cook until bubbles start to form around the edges, 2 to 3 minutes. Remove from the heat and stir in the Cheddar and Parmesan until the cheese is melted. Add the pasta and half the Brussels sprouts.

**4.** Serve warm, topped with the remaining Brussels sprouts and the chives.

# Pumpkin Crème Fraîche Deviled Eggs

**Makes 12 deviled eggs**

6 eggs

¼ cup [60 ml] Pumpkin &
White Bean Soup (page 51)

2 Tbsp crème fraîche

1 Tbsp Dijon mustard

¼ tsp salt

**Topping Options**

Chopped fresh dill

Small sage leaves

Smoked paprika

Candied Bacon (page 216)

Pickled Mustard Seeds
(page 213)

I love how easy it is to vary deviled eggs. When making these, I usually make a batch of traditional deviled eggs alongside to give guests a variety, and I serve them with an array of toppings for a visually interesting presentation.

1. Place the eggs in a single layer in a saucepan and cover with water. Bring to a boil over high heat and boil for 1 minute. Remove from the heat, cover, and let sit for 12 minutes. Drain the eggs and rinse under cold running water for 1 minute. Peel the eggs and halve them lengthwise. Transfer the yolks to a medium bowl and the whites to a serving platter cut-side up.

2. Use a fork to mash the yolks into a fine crumb. Add the soup, crème fraîche, mustard, and salt and mix until combined. Alternatively, for a smoother filling, you could blend the filling in a small food processor.

3. Spoon a heaping tsp of filling into each egg white, or transfer the filling to a zip-top bag, trim off the corner of the bag, and pipe the filling into the egg whites.

4. Top with dill, sage, a sprinkle of paprika, crumbled candied bacon, and/or pickled mustard seeds, if desired. Serve right away or cover and chill in the fridge until ready to serve. These are best enjoyed the same day.

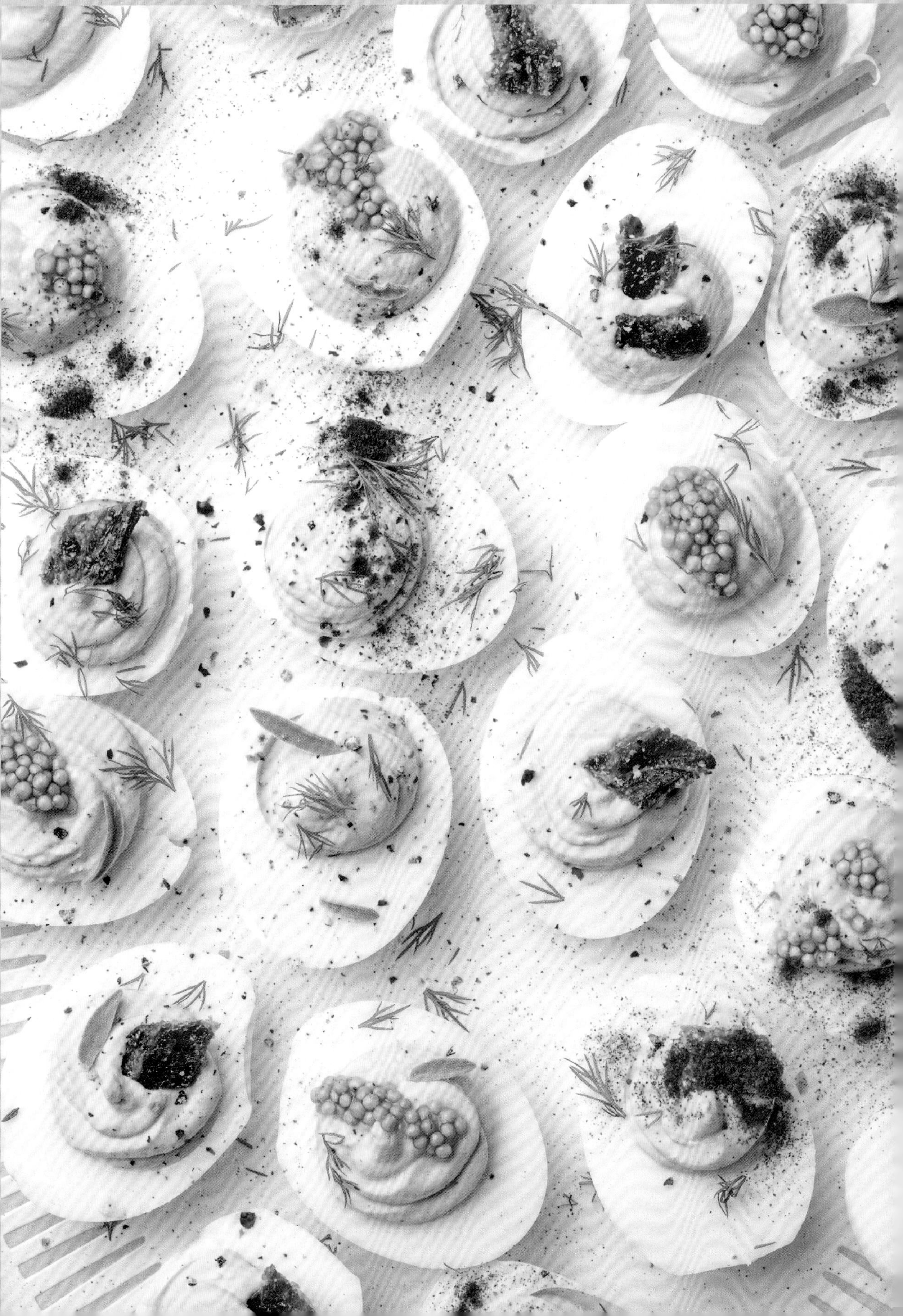

# Coconut Pumpkin Curry Red Lentil Stew

**Serves 6 to 8**

¼ cup [60 ml] olive oil or coconut oil

1 yellow onion, chopped

2 in [5 cm] piece fresh ginger, peeled and minced

4 garlic cloves, minced

2 cups [400 g] red lentils, rinsed

1 tsp curry powder

1 tsp red pepper flakes

½ Tbsp salt

½ tsp ground turmeric

4 cups [960 ml] Homemade Roasted Vegetable Broth (page 209) or store-bought low-sodium vegetable broth

One 15 oz [430 g] can pumpkin purée

One 14 oz [400 g] can coconut milk

½ Tbsp lime juice

Freshly ground black pepper

1 cup [12 g] fresh mint leaves

Plain yogurt and pita bread, for serving

~~~~~~~~~~

**Meat Suggestion**

Wyatt loves to sauté a few Spicy Shrimp (page 216) to stir into this soup.

**Quick Fix**

To bring new texture to your leftovers, add a few triangles of Honeyed Feta with Black & White Sesame Seeds (page 214) as a topping for your reheated soup.

Pumpkin helps fill out this soup with extra volume and nutrients without overpowering the coconut flavor. As written, this recipe is perfect for weeknight meals, but if you are wanting to create a richly over-the-top version as a starter for guests, feel free to add an additional can of coconut milk. I find this to be too rich as a main weeknight meal but absolutely divine as a small shooter serving.

1. In a large Dutch oven or pot over medium heat, warm the oil. Add the onion and sauté until soft and translucent, 5 to 7 minutes. Add the ginger and garlic and sauté until fragrant, 30 seconds. Add the lentils, curry powder, red pepper flakes, salt, and turmeric and sauté for 30 seconds more.

2. Add the vegetable broth, pumpkin, and coconut milk and stir to combine. Bring to a boil over high heat. Turn the heat down to medium-low and simmer until the lentils are cooked to your liking, 15 to 20 minutes.

3. Remove from the heat and stir in the lime juice. Taste and season with salt (I usually need to add an additional ½ tsp) and pepper as needed. Serve with dollops of yogurt, mint leaves, and pita bread.

☞ **Slow Cooker:** Follow step 1 as written. Transfer the mixture to a slow cooker and stir in the pumpkin, coconut milk, and 2½ cups [600 ml] vegetable broth (instead of 4 cups [960]) and cook on low for 4 hours or high for 2, stirring every hour or so. Proceed with the recipe from step 3.

☞ **Storing:** Store leftovers refrigerated in an airtight container for up to 3 days or freeze for up to 3 months.

# Lettuce Wraps with Cilantro-Lime Rice & Baked Tofu

**Serves 4**

### Baked Tofu

One 14 oz [400 g] package extra-firm tofu

1 Tbsp olive oil

2 tsp tamari or soy sauce

1 Tbsp cornstarch

### Cilantro-Lime Rice

2 Tbsp unsalted butter

1 shallot, minced

1 cup [200 g] basmati or other long-grain rice, rinsed

½ tsp salt

1 bunch fresh cilantro, chopped

Juice of ½ lime

1 tsp chili-garlic sauce, or 1 small fresh hot chile, such as jalapeño or serrano, diced

### Wraps

1½ cups [360 ml] Coconut Pumpkin Curry Red Lentil Stew (page 59)

1 carrot, peeled and cut into matchsticks

1 small red bell pepper, cored and cut into matchsticks

1 green onion, chopped

1 head iceberg lettuce or Bibb lettuce, leaves separated

The Coconut Pumpkin Curry Red Lentil Stew (page 59) is so packed with flavor, it makes a perfect sauce on these lettuce wraps. Wyatt likes to sauté some Spicy Shrimp (page 216) to go along with the tofu. Shredded Chicken (page 217) could also be a great meat option if your family prefers it.

1. **Make the tofu:** Preheat the oven to 400°F [200°C] and line a baking sheet with parchment paper. Drain the tofu and press excess water out by wrapping it in several layers of paper towel and then placing a heavy pan on it for at least 10 minutes.

2. Remove and discard the paper towels. Cut the tofu into equal pieces by cutting the slab into thirds, and then stack the pieces on top of each other and slice lengthwise again three times to create nine rectangular strips. Cut the strips into five pieces each to create bite-size rectangles. Place the tofu on the prepared baking sheet and toss with the oil and tamari, followed by the cornstarch. Bake for 20 to 25 minutes, tossing halfway through, or until it darkens a bit in color.

3. **Meanwhile, make the rice:** In a medium saucepan over medium heat, melt the butter. Add the shallot and sauté until softened and just starting to take on color, 3 to 5 minutes. Add the rice and sauté for 30 seconds, tossing to coat it completely in the butter. Add 1½ cups [360 ml] of water and the salt. Turn down the heat to medium-low and simmer, covered, until the liquid has absorbed, 17 to 20 minutes. Remove from the heat and let sit, covered, for an additional 10 minutes to steam. Use a fork or spatula to stir in the cilantro, lime juice, and chili-garlic sauce.

4. **Make the wraps:** Warm the stew in a small saucepan over medium heat, stirring often, until it reaches at least 165°F [75°C] and is simmering. Put the tofu, rice, stew, carrot, bell pepper, and green onion in separate serving bowls. Put the lettuce leaves on a plate for people to assemble their own wraps, topping each with tofu, veggies, and stew.

# Caramelized Cabbage Barley Stew

**Serves 4**

¼ cup [60 ml] olive oil

1 white onion, diced

2 garlic cloves, minced

1 large head green cabbage (about 1½ lb [680 g]), cored and thinly sliced

3 thyme sprigs

1 tsp salt

¼ tsp freshly ground black pepper

4 cups [960 ml] Homemade Roasted Vegetable Broth (page 209) or store-bought low-sodium vegetable broth

⅔ cup [130 g] pearled barley, rinsed

2 Tbsp champagne vinegar or white wine vinegar

⅓ cup [10 g] Parmesan cheese, plus more for serving

2 Tbsp unsalted butter

**Meat Suggestion**

Add in some Mini Meatballs (page 217) at serving time.

**Quick Fix**

Maybe I'm always just looking for an excuse to eat Polish dumplings, but I found that reheating the leftover soup and pouring it over cooked pierogi was the perfect way to give this humble soup new life the next day. If you want to make homemade, my family's pierogi recipe is in my first cookbook, *Vegetarian Heartland*; for a quick store-bought option, I love Kasia's Deli pierogi.

This quick, simple stew is my riff on Marcella Hazan's rice and smothered cabbage soup. As I was researching her soup, I kept seeing review after review in disbelief about how something so simple could be so flavorful and delicious. Needless to say, I had to try it and was not disappointed. If you don't have barley on hand, this soup is also delicious with farro or wheat berries, just make sure to adjust the time they cook depending on the package directions. Feel free to add more vegetable broth at the end if you'd like it to be more soupy than stewy.

1. In a large Dutch oven or stockpot over medium heat, warm the oil. Add the onion and sauté until translucent, about 7 minutes. Add the garlic and sauté until fragrant, 30 seconds. Add the cabbage, thyme, salt, and pepper and toss to coat the cabbage in oil. Cover, turn the heat down to medium-low, and cook, stirring often, until the cabbage has softened, about 30 minutes.

2. Add the vegetable broth, barley, and 1 Tbsp of the vinegar and bring to a simmer over high heat. Turn the heat down to medium-low and simmer, uncovered, until the barley is tender, about 25 minutes.

3. Remove from the heat and stir in the Parmesan, butter, and remaining 1 Tbsp of vinegar. Fish out the thyme sprigs and toss. The soup should be thick, but feel free to add water or more vegetable broth if you'd like it thinner. Taste and season with salt and pepper as needed.

☞ **Slow Cooker:** Sauté the onion and garlic in a pan as in step 1. Add to the slow cooker along with the cabbage, thyme, salt, and pepper and toss to coat the cabbage in oil. Cook on high for 3 hours, stirring every 30 minutes or so. Uncover, add 2 cups [480 ml] of vegetable broth, the barley, and 1 Tbsp of the vinegar and cook on high for another 3 hours or until the barley is cooked all the way through. Continue with the recipe at step 3.

☞ **Storing:** Store leftovers refrigerated in an airtight container for up to 3 days or freeze for up to 2 months.

# Chickpea Noodle Soup with Lemon & Dill

Serves 6

**Egg Noodles**

1½ cups [210 g] all-purpose flour

¼ tsp salt

2 eggs, lightly beaten

**Soup**

2 Tbsp olive oil

4 celery stalks, diced

2 carrots, peeled and sliced into coins

1 white onion, diced

2 garlic cloves, minced

Three 2 in [5 cm] strips lemon peel

1 tsp salt

¼ tsp freshly ground black pepper

¼ tsp red pepper flakes, plus more for serving

4 cups [960 ml] Homemade Roasted Vegetable Broth (page 209) or store-bought low-sodium vegetable broth

One 15 oz [430 g] can chickpeas, rinsed

2 bay leaves

2 Tbsp yellow miso

1½ Tbsp fresh lemon juice

¼ cup [3 g] chopped fresh dill

**Meat Suggestion**

Create a comforting chicken and noodle soup by adding Shredded Chicken (page 217) when you add in the lemon juice.

This is a delicious Sunday project for when it's too cold to be outside and you are craving something carb-y like homemade noodles. Technically you could add chicken to this soup to make it more traditional, but it is delicious as a vegetarian soup with hearty chickpeas, a burst of umami from the miso paste, and brightness from lemon and fresh dill.

Although I usually recommend you cook noodles separately from your soup to avoid soggy noodle leftovers, these homemade noodles get a lot of their flavor from being cooked in the broth, so I throw them right in. Also these noodles are a bit denser than store-bought ones, so I find they don't get as mushy the next day. You could always strain out the liquid before storing if you are planning to make the Egg Noodles with Chickpeas, Kale & Mascarpone (page 70) with your leftovers.

1. **Make the egg noodles:** Add the flour and salt to a food processor fitted with a blade attachment and pulse a few times to mix. Add the eggs and 1 Tbsp of water and pulse until a rice-size crumb forms. Use clean hands to gather the dough into a ball and knead it on a clean counter to form a smooth dough, about 30 seconds. Cover with plastic wrap and let rest for 30 minutes.

2. Divide the dough in half and keep the half you aren't using covered. Roll out the dough with a rolling pin into a rough square ⅛ in [4 mm] thick. Use a sharp knife or pizza cutter to cut roughly 2 by ½ in [5 cm by 13 mm] strips (these don't have to be exact). Set aside the strips in a bowl and repeat with the remaining dough.

continued ☞

**Quick Fix**

Add 1 cup [15 g] of your favorite hearty greens, chopped, to liven up this soup after reheating it the next day. My favorites are massaged kale with a little lemon juice or marinated radicchio (page 47).

**3.** **Make the soup:** In a large Dutch oven or stockpot over medium heat, warm the oil. Add the celery, carrot, and onion and sauté until softened, 7 to 10 minutes. Add the garlic, lemon peel, salt, pepper, and red pepper flakes and sauté until fragrant, 30 seconds. Add the vegetable broth, chickpeas, bay leaves, and 2 cups [475 ml] of water and bring to a boil over high heat. Lower the heat to medium-low and simmer for 15 minutes to develop flavor.

**4.** Add the noodles to the pot, cover, and simmer until the noodles are cooked all the way through, about 6 minutes.

**5.** Scoop out 1 cup [240 ml] of broth from the soup and whisk the miso into it. Add back into the soup along with the lemon juice and stir to combine. Taste and season with salt and pepper as needed. Serve, topped with the dill and more red pepper flakes.

☞ **Pressure Cooker:** Prepare the noodles as instructed in steps 1 and 2. Use the sauté function to cook the aromatics as in step 3. Add the vegetable broth, chickpeas, bay leaves, and 1½ cups [360 ml] water (instead of 2 cups [480 ml]). Pressure cook on high for 5 minutes, then quick release. Turn the sauté function back on and add in the noodles. Simmer until cooked all the way through, about 6 minutes. Proceed with the recipe starting with step 5.

☞ **Storing:** Store leftovers refrigerated in an airtight container for up to 2 days. I do not recommend freezing this soup, as the noodles won't hold up well.

# Egg Noodles with Chickpeas, Kale & Mascarpone

**Serves 2 or 4 with a side**

2 Tbsp olive oil

1 yellow onion, diced

3 garlic cloves, minced

3 cups [720 ml] Chickpea Noodle Soup with Lemon & Dill (page 67), drained and rinsed

2 Calabrian chile peppers in oil (more if you like a lot of spice!), chopped

2 tsp tomato paste

1 tsp sugar

½ tsp salt

¼ tsp freshly ground black pepper, plus more for serving

1 cup [15 g] chopped kale

4 oz [115 g] mascarpone

1 oz [30 g] Parmesan cheese, grated, plus shaved Parmesan for serving

You made homemade noodles yesterday (page 67; go you!), so treat yourself today with this indulgent pasta dish that uses rich mascarpone for the sauce and spicy Calabrian chiles for heat. Use more if you like it spicy or serve some on the side to let people choose.

1. In a large heavy-bottomed pan over medium heat, heat the oil. Add the onion and cook until translucent, about 5 minutes. Add the garlic and cook until fragrant, about 1 minute. Add the soup, Calabrian chiles, tomato paste, sugar, salt, and pepper and cook until the noodles are warmed through and any excess liquid has been cooked off, 3 to 5 minutes.

2. Add the kale and sauté for 20 seconds (I like the kale to still have a little bite to it; cook it for longer if you like your kale softer). Remove from the heat and stir in the mascarpone and Parmesan. Serve warm, topped with shaved Parmesan and black pepper.

# Smoked Paprika Tortilla Soup

Serves 4 to 6

4 Tbsp [60 ml] olive oil

1 red onion, diced

1 red bell pepper, diced

1 jalapeño, minced

4 garlic cloves, minced

1 Tbsp chili powder

1¼ tsp salt

1 tsp ground cumin

1 tsp smoked paprika

¼ tsp cayenne pepper

4 cups [960 ml] Homemade Roasted Vegetable Broth (page 209) or store-bought low-sodium vegetable broth

Two 15 oz [430 g] cans black beans, rinsed

One 28 oz [800 g] can crushed fire-roasted tomatoes

1 cup [140 g] frozen corn

¼ cup [10 g] chopped fresh cilantro, plus more for serving

1 Tbsp fresh lime juice

5 corn tortillas, cut into 2 by ½ in [5 cm by 13 mm] strips

Sliced avocado, sour cream, and lime wedges, for serving

**Meat Suggestion**

Mix in some Shredded Chicken (page 217) at the end to bulk up the protein.

This simplified Mexican soup is served with crispy tortilla strips. It's traditionally made with corn tortillas, but you could use flour tortillas if that's what you have on hand. I also bake the tortilla chips in the oven instead of frying, which I find to be a bit more weeknight-friendly in terms of cleanup. You still need to watch them closely; toss them often toward the end of their baking time so they don't burn.

1. Preheat the oven to 375°F [190°C].

2. In a large stockpot or Dutch oven over medium heat, warm 2 Tbsp of the oil. Add the onion, bell pepper, and jalapeño and sauté until softened, 5 to 7 minutes. Add the garlic, chili powder, 1 tsp of the salt, the cumin, paprika, and cayenne and sauté until fragrant, 30 seconds.

3. Add the vegetable broth, beans, tomatoes and their juice, and corn and bring to a simmer over high heat. Lower the heat to medium-low and simmer for 30 minutes. Remove from the heat and stir in the cilantro and lime juice. Taste and add salt as needed.

4. Meanwhile, toss the tortilla strips with the remaining 2 Tbsp of oil and spread in an even layer on a baking sheet. Bake until golden, 15 to 17 minutes, tossing halfway through and again toward the end of the cooking.

5. Serve the soup topped with the tortilla strips, avocado, sour cream, lime wedges, and more cilantro.

☞ **Slow Cooker:** Follow the directions through sautéing the spices in step 2. Add 3 cups [720 ml] vegetable broth (instead of 4 cups [960 ml]) to the pot to deglaze it and then transfer everything in the pot to a slow cooker. Add the beans, tomatoes and their juice, and corn and cook on high for 4 hours or on low for 8. About 30 minutes before the soup is ready, make the tortilla strips as described in step 4 and continue with the recipe.

☞ **Storing:** Store leftovers refrigerated in an airtight container for up to 3 days or freeze for up to 2 months.

# Nachos

**Serves 4 as a main,
8 to 10 as a snack**

10 oz [280 g] tortilla chips

1½ cups [360 ml] Smoked
Paprika Tortilla Soup (page 73)

1 Tbsp unsalted butter

1 Tbsp all-purpose flour

1 cup [240 ml] whole milk

4 oz [115 g] shredded pepper
Jack cheese

½ tsp smoked paprika

¼ tsp salt

**Topping Options**

Pickled jalapeños

Sour cream

Guacamole or avocado slices

Chopped chives

Pico de gallo

Cilantro leaves

Hot sauce

I probably make a batch of nachos for dinner more than anything else on weeknights when I'm short for time. Wyatt loves to top his half of the nachos with Shredded Chicken (page 217). You can also swap in waffle fries if you want to make these loaded fries instead!

**1.** Preheat the oven to 350°F [180°C]

**2.** Spread out the tortilla chips on a baking sheet. Drain the liquid from the soup and spread the solid pieces from the soup over the tortilla chips. Bake for 10 minutes or until warm.

**3.** Meanwhile, in a medium skillet over medium heat, melt the butter and whisk in the flour. Slowly whisk in the milk and bring to a simmer, stirring often. The sauce should thicken up slightly within 1 to 2 minutes; when it does, remove it from the heat. Whisk in the pepper Jack, smoked paprika, and salt.

**4.** Drizzle the cheese sauce over the warmed nachos and top with an array of toppings.

# Butternut Squash & Mushroom Lasagna Soup

**Serves 6**

4 Tbsp [55 g] unsalted butter

1 yellow onion, diced

4 garlic cloves, minced

¼ cup [35 g] all-purpose flour

4 cups [960 ml] Homemade Roasted Vegetable Broth (page 209) or store-bought low-sodium vegetable broth

1 lb [455 g] butternut squash, cut into ½ in [13 mm] cubes (about 3½ cups)

8 oz [230 g] white button mushrooms, sliced

1 Tbsp chopped fresh sage

1 tsp red pepper flakes

8 lasagna noodles, broken in half

1 cup [240 ml] whole milk

Salt

Freshly ground black pepper

4 oz [115 g] mozzarella cheese, shredded

½ cup [15 g] grated Parmesan cheese

### Meat Suggestion

Shredded Chicken (page 217) can be added to the soup after removing it from the heat and before stirring in the milk.

### Quick Fix

Stir a few handfuls of baby spinach into the reheated soup right before serving or whip up a batch of Citrus-Artichoke White Pesto (page 214) to stir into your leftovers.

This is a very hearty soup for when you are craving carbs and cheese but also want them served with a few vegetables. If you are feeling extra enthusiastic, brown a few tablespoons of butter and drizzle it over the top of each bowl. When I'm not in the mood to battle with peeling and chopping a butternut squash for this soup, I use sweet potatoes in their place. As with many of the other soup recipes in this book that involve pasta, I cook the lasagna noodles separately so that they don't get soggy when left over. If you're planning to eat all this soup at one meal, then you could cook them right into the soup.

1. In a large Dutch oven over medium heat, melt the butter. Add the onion and sauté until very soft, 5 to 7 minutes. Add the garlic and sauté until fragrant but not yet browning, 30 seconds. Add the flour and whisk for 1 minute, until the flour darkens slightly and smells nutty.

2. Add the vegetable broth, squash, mushrooms, sage, and red pepper flakes and bring to a boil over high heat. Turn down the heat to medium-low and simmer until the squash is tender and easily pierced with a fork, 15 to 20 minutes.

3. Meanwhile, bring a large pot of salted water to a boil over high heat. Cook the lasagna noodles according to the package directions and drain.

4. Remove the soup from the heat and stir in the milk. Taste and season with salt and pepper as needed. Divide the soup among serving bowls and nestle the lasagna noodles into the soup. Top each bowl with mozzarella and Parmesan and serve right away.

☞ **Pressure Cooker:** Using the sauté function, follow step 1 through toasting the flour. Add 3 cups [720 ml] vegetable broth (instead of 4 cups [960 ml]), along with the squash, mushrooms, sage, and red pepper flakes. Pressure cook on high for 5 minutes, then quick release. Let cool slightly until the steam has mostly subsided, about 5 minutes. Continue with the recipe from step 3.

☞ **Storing:** Store leftover soup and pasta refrigerated in separate airtight containers for up to 3 days. I do not recommend freezing this soup due to the dairy and pasta.

# Chili Cook-Off

After avoiding them for years, Wyatt and I finally got into watching competition cooking shows during the pandemic's stay-at-home order. Once we were able to socialize again, we had a blast hosting our own little competitions in our backyard! A chili cook-off is a classic—here are a few tips for hosting your own.

Before the event, you'll want to make numbered signs for each chili and a ballot for people to vote with. Stock up on tortilla chips, and make a few batches of cornbread for guests to enjoy between chili bites. Have disposable paper bowls or cups and silverware ready. Ask your guests to bring a slow cooker full of their favorite chili (this will keep the chili hot, since you likely won't have enough burners to warm them all up at the same time) and a ladle. To keep it anonymous, assign each chili a number when it arrives. Line up the cookers on your kitchen counter, so guests can sample each and use their ballot to vote. Once everyone has finished their ballots, tally up the votes and announce the winner. If you want to really go all out, you can also assign three judges to pick their favorite chili, *Top Chef* style, explaining what they did and didn't like about each chili, before announcing the winners according to the judges and by popular vote. Some fun prizes could be a chili or soup cookbook (maybe this one?), a "Chili Cook-Off Winner" embroidered apron, or a gift card for a local coffee or ice cream shop.

SMELL

FLAVOR

TEXTURE

HEAT

TOTAL

# Carrot-Orange-Ginger Soup

**Serves 4**

2 Tbsp olive oil,
plus more for serving

1½ lb [680 g] orange carrots,
peeled and cut into 1 in [2.5 cm]
pieces

1 white onion, diced

2 celery stalks, cut into 1 in
[2.5 cm] pieces

5 garlic cloves, minced

2 in [5 cm] piece fresh ginger,
peeled and roughly chopped

1 tsp salt

½ tsp ground cumin

¼ tsp ground coriander

¼ tsp ground turmeric

⅛ tsp cayenne pepper

4 cups [960 ml] Homemade
Roasted Vegetable Broth
(page 209) or store-bought low-
sodium vegetable broth

1 bay leaf

Grated zest and juice of 1 navel
orange

½ tsp maple syrup (optional)

¼ cup [60 ml] whole milk or
heavy cream

Freshly ground black pepper

Roasted pepitas and chopped
fresh cilantro, for serving
(optional)

**Meat Suggestion**

Sprinkle crumbled Candied Bacon
(page 216) on top when serving.

**Quick Fix**

Swirl in some Green
Tahini (page 212)
and sprinkle with
black and white
sesame seeds for
a visual stunner of
a soup!

Is this soup based on my favorite ginger-turmeric carrot-orange juice from my local juice bar? Maybe . . . and I have no regrets about it. I use very small amounts of spices in this recipe to add depth without overpowering any of the sweet carrot or bright orange notes. Depending on how sweet your carrots are, you may need to add a touch of maple syrup at the end to bring out their sweetness, so make sure to taste and adjust to your liking. I always have whole milk on hand, so it's what I use here to round out the flavor, but you can make it even richer with heavy cream. Or make it vegan by swapping in canned coconut milk, which will alter the flavor but still be delicious!

1. In a Dutch oven over medium heat, heat the oil. Add the carrots, onion, and celery and sauté until softened, 7 to 10 minutes. Add the garlic, ginger, salt, cumin, coriander, turmeric, and cayenne and sauté until fragrant, 30 seconds.

2. Add the vegetable broth and bay leaf and bring to a boil over high heat. Cover, turn down the heat to low, and simmer until the carrots are tender, about 20 minutes.

3. Remove from the heat, remove the bay leaf, and use an immersion blender to blend until smooth. Whisk in the orange zest, orange juice, maple syrup (if using), and milk. Taste and season with salt and pepper as needed.

4. Divide among four bowls and drizzle with a little oil. Sprinkle with pepitas and/or cilantro, if desired. Serve warm.

☞ **Pressure Cooker:** Using the sauté function on your pressure cooker, follow the instructions in step 1 for sautéing the aromatics and spices. Add 3 cups [320 ml] vegetable broth (instead of 4 cups [960 ml]) along with the bay leaf. Pressure cook on high for 7 minutes, then quick release. Let the soup cool slightly, about 3 minutes, or until the steam has subsided substantially. Continue with the recipe from step 3.

☞ **Storing:** Store leftovers refrigerated in an airtight container for up to 4 days. If you want to freeze, don't add the milk or cream into the portion you are freezing, and freeze in an airtight container for up to 3 months.

# Savory Sesame-Carrot Oatmeal

### Serves 2

1 tsp unsalted butter

1 garlic clove, minced

1 tsp ground ginger

1 cup [240 ml] Homemade Roasted Vegetable Broth (page 209) or store-bought low-sodium vegetable broth

1 cup [240 ml] Carrot-Orange-Ginger Soup (page 85)

1 cup [100 g] quick-cooking rolled oats

¼ tsp salt

1 green onion, thinly sliced, or 1 Tbsp thinly sliced fresh chives

2 tsp sesame oil

2 tsp toasted sesame seeds

Freshly ground black pepper

2 soft-boiled eggs, peeled and halved, or 2 fried eggs (optional)

I often turn to oatmeal for breakfast on chilly mornings, and I love to mix up my usual cinnamon flavor with a savory version now and then. This dish is packed full of vegetables thanks to the leftover Carrot-Orange-Ginger Soup (page 85) and elevated with sesame oil and green onions. Although it's not necessary, if you're wanting a heartier breakfast, serve this with a soft-boiled or fried egg.

**1.** In a small saucepan over medium heat, melt the butter. Add the garlic and ginger and sauté until fragrant, 30 seconds. Add the vegetable broth and soup and bring to a boil. Lower the heat to medium-low and add the oats and salt. Cover and simmer until the oats are cooked all the way through, about 3 minutes, stirring every minute or so to keep the oats from sticking to the pan.

**2.** Remove from the heat and divide the oatmeal between two bowls. Top each bowl with half of the green onions, 1 tsp of the sesame oil, 1 tsp of the sesame seeds, and a grind of black pepper. Top each bowl with an egg (if using) and enjoy right away.

# Potato & Pea Stew with Indian Spices

**Serves 4 to 6**

2 Tbsp ghee

1 white onion, chopped

4 garlic cloves, smashed and peeled

1 in [2.5 cm] piece fresh ginger, peeled and roughly chopped

1 Tbsp yellow mustard seeds

1 tsp ground turmeric

1 tsp ground coriander

½ tsp ground cardamom

2 lb [910 g] Yukon gold potatoes, peeled and cut into 1 in [2.5 cm] cubes

One 14½ oz [415 g] can diced tomatoes, drained

1 fresh green chile, such as serrano, minced (remove the seeds if you don't like heat)

½ Tbsp salt

10 oz [280 g] frozen peas

1 Tbsp fresh lime juice, plus lime wedges for serving

Fresh cilantro leaves, for serving

## Meat Suggestion

Shredded Chicken (page 217) or even Spicy Shrimp (page 216) could be added to this soup if you are feeling it.

### Quick Fix

Swirl a few tablespoons of Green Apple-Mint Chutney (page 212) into each bowl of soup right before serving.

Wyatt gets very cranky if we don't get our weekly Indian takeout from his favorite place in town. Inspired by a few of my favorite vegetarian options there, this starchy stew is delicious served with a side of Quick Yogurt Flatbread (page 235) and some rice. Remove the seeds from the green chile if you don't like a lot of spice.

**1.** In a large stockpot over medium heat, melt 1 Tbsp of the ghee. Add the onion, garlic, and ginger and sauté just until the onions have softened, 5 to 7 minutes. Add the mustard seeds, turmeric, coriander, and cardamom and sauté until fragrant, 30 seconds. Add 2 cups [480 ml] water, transfer the mixture to a blender (or use an immersion blender), and blend until smooth (it's OK if the mustard seeds don't all break down). Set aside.

**2.** Rinse the stockpot and melt the remaining 1 Tbsp of ghee in it over medium heat. Add the potatoes, tomatoes, and chile and sauté until most of the moisture has been cooked out of the tomatoes, about 5 minutes.

**3.** Add the spice mixture from the blender, 3 cups [720 ml] of water, and the salt to the pot and bring to a boil over high heat. Lower the heat to medium-low and simmer until the potatoes are easily pierced with a fork, 15 minutes. Use a fork to smash a few of the potatoes to release their starches and thicken the soup up a bit. Stir in the peas and simmer until heated through, about 5 minutes.

**4.** Remove from the heat and stir in the lime juice. Taste and season with salt and lime juice as needed. Serve topped with cilantro.

☞ **Slow Cooker:** Follow the directions above through step 2. Transfer the potato mixture, blended spice mixture, and 2 cups [480 ml] water to a slow cooker and cook on high for 4 to 6 hours. When there is 1 hour left of cooking, use a fork to gently smash a few of the potatoes, and add the peas. Continue with the recipe from step 4.

☞ **Storing:** Store leftovers refrigerated in an airtight container for up to 3 days. This can be frozen for up to 3 months, but it could alter the texture of the soup, so I don't recommend it.

# Fritters with Green Apple–Mint Chutney Yogurt Sauce

**Serves 2 as a main
or 4 as a starter or side**

2 cups [480 ml] Potato &
Pea Stew with Indian Spices
(page 91)

1 egg, lightly beaten

¼ cup [35 g] all-purpose flour

Ghee, for frying

½ cup [120 g] plain whole-milk
yogurt

¼ cup [75 g] Green Apple–Mint
Chutney (page 212)

Salt

Freshly ground black pepper

If you don't feel like making your own apple–mint chutney, you could use store-bought mango chutney to bring a little sweetness to these savory fritters.

**I.** Put the soup in a fine-mesh strainer with a large bowl underneath it. Transfer to the fridge and drain for at least 30 minutes. Use the back of a spatula to press out as much liquid as possible. Discard the liquid and transfer the solids into a large bowl.

**2.** Use a potato masher or a fork to smash the drained soup into a thick mashed-potato consistency (it's OK if not all the peas are smashed, but all the tomatoes and potatoes should be). Add the egg and flour and use a spatula to mix until completely combined. The consistency should be wet but thick enough that it doesn't run when you pull the mixture away from the sides of the bowl (think thick mashed-potatoes consistency).

**3.** Line a plate with two layers of paper towels. In a small skillet over medium heat, melt enough ghee to cover the bottom of the skillet (for me this was 1 tsp per patty). Working in batches, use a ¼ cup [60 ml] measuring cup to scoop out a portion of the mixture and add it to the hot pan. Use the back of the measuring cup to gently smash the patty down. You can add several patties to the pan at once, but make sure not to overcrowd it. None of the patties should be touching. Fry the patties until golden brown on both sides and cooked all the way through, about 3 minutes on each side. Transfer to the prepared plate and continue with the rest of the fritter mixture.

**4.** In a small bowl, whisk together the yogurt and chutney. Taste and season with salt and pepper as needed. Serve the fritters warm with a dollop of the yogurt sauce.

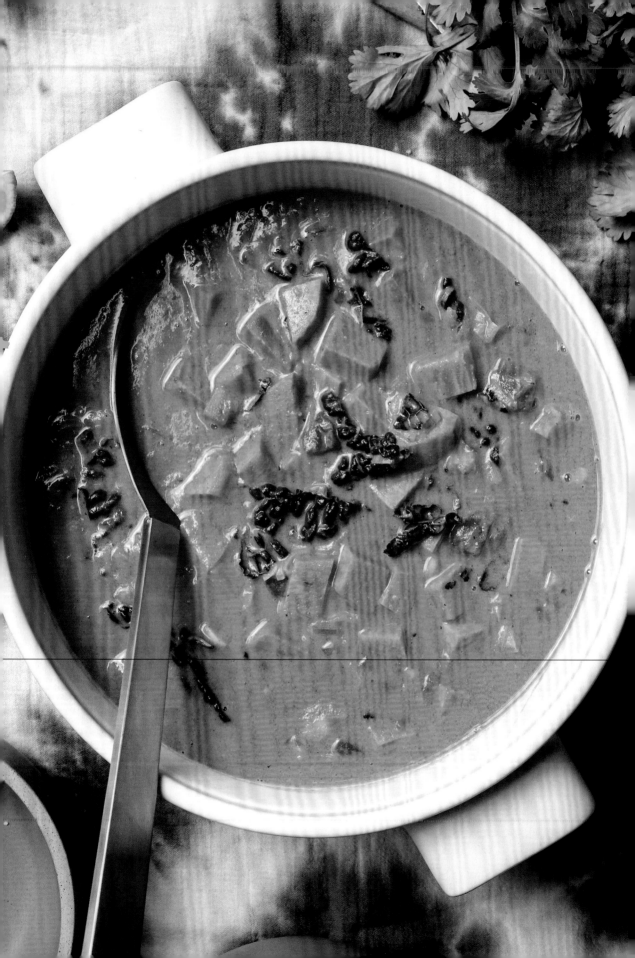

# Sweet Potato & Leek Peanut Stew

Serves 4 to 6

2 Tbsp olive oil, peanut oil, or coconut oil

1 medium leek or 2 small leeks, thinly sliced

2 medium sweet potatoes (about 260 g [4.5 oz]), peeled and cut into ½ in [13 mm] cubes

¼ cup [55 g] tomato paste

1 in [2.5 cm] piece fresh ginger, peeled and minced

1 serrano chile, minced

1 tsp salt

1 tsp ground cumin

1 tsp ground coriander

½ tsp ground turmeric

3 cups [720 ml] Homemade Roasted Vegetable Broth (page 209) or store-bought low-sodium vegetable broth

One 14 oz [400 g] can coconut milk

One 14 oz [400 g] can diced fire-roasted tomatoes

½ cup [130 g] creamy peanut butter

2 cups [30 g] packed chopped kale

1 Tbsp fresh lime juice, plus more for seasoning

½ cup [70 g] chopped roasted peanuts

¼ cup [10 g] chopped fresh cilantro

This soup takes inspiration from both African peanut stew and Indian curry—rich from peanut butter, loaded with spices, and creamy from coconut milk. If you have peanut oil on hand, you can substitute it for the olive oil in this recipe. In the summer, try swapping in zucchini and red bell pepper for the leeks and sweet potatoes for a lighter version of this hearty stew.

1. In a large stockpot over medium heat, heat the oil. Add the leek and sauté until softened, about 7 minutes. Add the sweet potatoes, tomato paste, ginger, serrano, salt, cumin, coriander, and turmeric and sauté until fragrant, 30 seconds.

2. Stir in the vegetable broth, coconut milk, and tomatoes and their juice and bring to a boil over high heat. Lower the heat to medium-low and simmer until the sweet potatoes are easily pierced with a fork, about 20 minutes.

3. Scoop out ½ cup [120 ml] of the broth from the soup into a small bowl and whisk the peanut butter into it until completely combined. Whisk the peanut butter mixture back into the soup. Remove from the heat and stir in the kale and lime juice. Taste and season with salt and lime as needed. Serve, topped with peanuts and cilantro.

☞ **Pressure Cooker:** Use the sauté function on the pressure cooker to follow the directions in step 1. Stir in the coconut milk, tomatoes and their juice, and 2 cups [480 ml] vegetable broth (instead of 3 cups [720 ml]). Pressure cook on high for 5 minutes, then quick release. Continue with the recipes starting at step 3.

☞ **Storing:** Store leftovers refrigerated in an airtight container for up to 3 days. I do not recommend freezing this due to the coconut milk.

## Meat Suggestion

Shredded Chicken (page 217) could be mixed in at the end. Note that you may need to add a bit more vegetable broth when adding the chicken to make up for the extra volume the chicken will add.

### Quick Fix

Serve over roasted broccoli and brown or white rice. When reheating, add a little water to thin the soup out, as it will have thickened in the fridge overnight.

# Spicy Peanut Noodle Stir-Fry

### Serves 4

6 oz [170 g] stir-fry noodles

2 cups [480 ml] Sweet Potato &
Leek Peanut Stew (page 95),
drained

1 Tbsp fresh lime juice

2 tsp honey

2 tsp rice vinegar

1 tsp chili-garlic sauce,
such as sambal oelek,
or red pepper flakes

1 tsp sesame oil

1 Tbsp olive, peanut, or
coconut oil

2 cups [120 g] shredded red
cabbage (from about
½ small head)

2 red bell peppers,
cut into strips

2 carrots, peeled and
cut into matchsticks

1 cup [65 g] snap peas

½ tsp salt

2 garlic cloves, minced

1 in [2.5 cm] piece fresh ginger,
peeled and minced

Chopped dry-roasted peanuts
and chopped fresh cilantro,
for serving

I love making this stir-fry on busy weeknights because it comes together quickly. If you know you'll be short on time when making this, you could even chop up the veggies the night before and store them in an airtight container in the fridge so they are all ready to stir-fry the next evening.

**1.** Bring a large pot of salted water to a boil over high heat. Add the stir-fry noodles and cook according to the package directions. Drain and set aside.

**2.** Meanwhile, in a small bowl, whisk together the stew, ½ cup [120 ml] of water, the lime juice, honey, vinegar, garlic chili sauce, and sesame oil.

**3.** In a large skillet, warm the olive oil over medium-high heat. Add the cabbage, bell peppers, carrots, snap peas, and salt and sauté until the vegetables have started to soften but still have a slight bite to them, about 7 minutes. Add the garlic and ginger and sauté until fragrant, 30 seconds.

**4.** Add the noodles and the sauce and sauté until everything is coated in the sauce and the sauce has thickened, 3 to 5 minutes. Top with peanuts and cilantro and serve right away.

# Roasted Root Vegetable & Dumpling Soup

**Serves 6 to 8**

### Roasted Vegetables

3 lb [1.4 kg] assorted root vegetables, such as leeks, carrots, Yukon gold potatoes, sweet potatoes, rutabaga, and turnips, cut into 1 in [2.5 cm] pieces

2 Tbsp olive oil

½ tsp salt

### Dumplings

1½ cups [210 g] all-purpose flour

½ tsp salt

½ tsp baking powder

½ tsp baking soda

¼ tsp freshly ground black pepper

½ cup [120 ml] whole milk

1 egg

2 Tbsp unsalted butter, melted and cooled

### Soup

1 Tbsp olive oil

1 yellow onion, diced

3 garlic cloves, minced

½ tsp salt

4 cups [960 ml] Homemade Roasted Vegetable Broth (page 209) or store-bought low-sodium vegetable broth

½ Tbsp chopped fresh tarragon, plus more for serving

Freshly ground black pepper

Chopped fresh chives, for serving (optional)

### Meat Suggestion

Add Mini Meatballs (page 217) to the soup right before serving.

I developed this recipe in honor of my Oma who, whenever we get on the topic of food, insists that there is nothing better than a simple meal of "roasted root vegetables." Although I can already guarantee that the addition of dumplings is more than she will want to fuss over, I made this recipe with simplicity in mind. I kept it as versatile as possible with the option to use a variety of whichever root vegetables you might have on hand (think leeks, carrots, potatoes, rutabaga, and so on). With that being said, I would suggest steering clear of red beets in this recipe since they would color the soup an unappetizing gray.

The addition of fresh tarragon at the end brings a brightness to this dish that I would find slightly lacking without. Just remember that a little goes a long way with this pungent, licorice-flavored herb! If you aren't a fan, you could substitute finely chopped chives instead.

1. **Make the roasted vegetables:** Preheat the oven to 400°F [200°C] and line two baking sheets with parchment paper. In a large bowl, toss the root vegetables with the oil and salt. Divide the vegetable between the baking sheets and roast for 30 minutes, or until the vegetables are easily pierced with a fork and starting to brown.

2. **Meanwhile, make the dumplings:** In a medium bowl, whisk together the flour, salt, baking powder, baking soda, and pepper. Make a well in the center of the dry ingredients and add the milk, egg, and butter. Starting in the center, whisk the wet ingredients together and then fold the dry ingredients into the wet ones until no dry bits remain and a shaggy dough has formed. Transfer to the fridge to keep chilled until ready to use.

continued ☞

**3. Make the soup:** When there is 5 minutes left for the veggies to roast, warm the oil in a large Dutch oven over medium heat. Add the onion and sauté until soft and translucent, 5 minutes. Add the garlic and salt and sauté until fragrant, 30 seconds.

**4.** Scrape the roasted veggies into the Dutch oven with the onions. Add the vegetable broth and 2 cups [480 ml] of water and bring to a boil over high heat. Scoop twelve even spoonfuls of dumpling dough into the soup, cover, and turn the heat down to medium-low. Simmer, covered, until the dumplings are cooked through, about 15 minutes.

**5.** Remove from the heat and stir in the tarragon. Taste and season with salt and pepper as needed. Serve with more tarragon and chives, if desired.

☞ **Pressure Cooker:** Follow the directions through step 2. When there is 5 minutes left for the veggies to roast, use the sauté function on the pressure cooker to sauté the aromatics as in step 3. Scrape the roasted veggies into the pressure cooker and add the vegetable broth and 1 cup [240 ml] of water. Scoop twelve even spoonfuls of dumpling dough into the soup. Pressure cook on high for 7 minutes, then quick release. When the steam clears, use two spoons to gently break apart the dumplings (they will have stuck together slightly but should still have held their shape). Continue with the recipe from step 5.

☞ **Storing:** Store leftovers refrigerated in an airtight container for up to 3 days. I do not recommend freezing this soup.

**Quick Fix**

Make a batch of Cider-Mustard Glaze (page 211) to drizzle over your soup after you've reheated it. If you are a fan of sweet and savory, you are going to love this because this slightly sweet glaze plays beautifully with this otherwise very savory soup.

# Dumpling Frittata with Gruyère

**Serves 4**

1 Tbsp olive oil

1 shallot, diced

2 garlic cloves, minced

2 cups [480 ml] vegetables from Roasted Root Vegetable & Dumpling Soup (page 101), rinsed and drained

2 dumplings from Roasted Root Vegetable & Dumpling Soup (page 101), quartered

2½ oz [70 g] Gruyère cheese, shredded

8 eggs

¾ cup [180 ml] whole milk

¼ cup [60 ml] heavy cream

2 tsp fresh thyme

½ tsp salt

¼ tsp freshly ground black pepper

8 oz [230 g] ricotta

Fresh parsley and red pepper flakes, for serving

Dumplings in . . . a frittata? Although this may sound weird at first, we add bread to eggs all the time, and a dumpling is made out of the same ingredients, so I figured why not? The result is irresistible—a vegetable-heavy egg dish speckled with pillowy savory doughy bites.

To repurpose your stew, remove the dumplings and vegetables from the liquid. Make sure to drain and rinse the vegetables well. Your dumplings will have become rather big when they were boiled, so quarter them to create bite-size doughy pieces for the frittata.

1. Preheat the oven to 400°F [200°C].

2. In a 10 in [25 cm] ovenproof skillet over medium heat, warm the oil. Add the shallot and sauté until softened, 2 to 3 minutes. Add the garlic and sauté until fragrant, 30 seconds. Add the leftover vegetables and sauté for another 30 seconds to let any excess moisture on the veggies cook off. Remove from the heat and nestle the eight dumpling pieces among the veggies. Sprinkle with half of the Gruyère.

3. In a medium bowl, whisk together the eggs, milk, cream, thyme, salt, and pepper. Pour over the veggies and cheese, using a spatula to mix the egg mixture around to make sure it has covered all the veggies. Dollop heaping spoonfuls of ricotta into the egg mixture. Sprinkle the remaining Gruyère over the top.

4. Bake for 20 to 25 minutes, or until the eggs are completely set. Turn the boiler on and broil until the top has started to brown, 1 to 2 minutes, watching closely to make sure it doesn't burn. Sprinkle with parsley and red pepper flakes and serve warm.

# French Onion Soup

Serves 8 to 10

2 Tbsp unsalted butter

1 Tbsp olive oil

3 lb [1.4 kg] white onions, sliced (see headnote)

1 tsp salt

1 cup [240 ml] dry white wine

2 Tbsp all-purpose flour

2 tsp fresh thyme

1 tsp onion powder

½ tsp garlic powder

6 cups [1.4 L] Homemade Roasted Vegetable Broth (page 209) or store-bought low-sodium vegetable broth

1½ Tbsp tamari or low-sodium soy sauce

1 tsp vegetarian Worcestershire sauce

1 Tbsp dry sherry

1 loaf French bread or baguette (about 6 oz [170 g]), torn into bite-size pieces

6 oz [170 g] Gruyère cheese, shredded

Freshly ground black pepper

Chopped fresh chives, for serving

## Meat Suggestion

Use beef broth (instead of vegetable) in this recipe for a more traditional flavor. If you do this, you can skip the Worcestershire and tamari sauce, and I'd recommend cutting back the salt a bit until you taste and season at the end.

This was my all-time favorite soup growing up. Since most restaurants use beef broth to make it, when I stopped eating meat as a teenager I quickly realized that I needed to create my own recipe. To replace the rich and deep beef broth that is usually associated with this soup, I add some umami and salty punch to the mix with vegetarian Worcestershire sauce and tamari. The splash of sherry really does add to the flavor, so I recommend not skipping if you can.

I used to always cut my onions as thin as I could so they would caramelize faster, but I've learned through trial and error that this is a mistake. You want the onions to be evenly sliced but not so thin that they will lose all texture and dissolve into the soup.

**1.** In a large stockpot or Dutch oven over medium heat, melt the butter and warm the oil. Add the onions and ½ tsp of the salt, cover, and cook for 5 minutes. Remove the lid and cook, stirring often, until golden brown and caramelized, 45 minutes to 1 hour.

**2.** Add the white wine and cook over medium heat for 5 to 10 minutes, until most of the wine has been absorbed. Add the flour, thyme, onion powder, garlic powder, and remaining ½ tsp of salt and stir to coat the onions with the spices and flour. Add the vegetable broth, tamari, and Worcestershire, raise the heat to medium-high, and bring to a simmer. Then cover, lower the heat to medium-low, and simmer for at least 30 minutes to develop flavor.

**3.** Remove from the heat and stir in the sherry. Once cool enough to sample, taste and season with salt and sherry as needed.

**4.** Preheat the broiler on high. Divide the soup among eight ovenproof ramekins (or however many people you are serving) and top each bowl with torn bread, Gruyère, and a grind of pepper. Carefully place the bowls on a baking sheet and broil for 1 to 2 minutes, or until the cheese has melted and is browning (watch closely, as broiler time will vary). Sprinkle with chives and serve warm.

☞ **Storing:** Remove any bread topping (it will get soggy) and discard. Store leftovers refrigerated in an airtight container for up to 3 days or freeze (without the bread or Gruyère) for up to 2 months.

# French Onion Strata Bake

**Serves 6**

2 cups [480 ml] French Onion Soup (page 107)

1 large loaf French bread, cut into 1 in [2.5 cm] pieces

1½ cups [360 ml] whole milk

6 eggs

1 Tbsp Dijon mustard

2 tsp fresh thyme

½ tsp salt

6 oz [170 g] Gruyère cheese, shredded

Freshly ground black pepper

One of my favorite ways to use up old bread is to make a bread pudding out of it, and this savory caramelized onion one is my current go-to. I wanted to highlight the flavors of the French onion soup with this, but you are welcome to add other veggies (spinach, roasted sweet potato pieces, bell pepper slices, and so on) and herbs (put hearty ones like rosemary into the bake and save softer herbs like parsley or dill for topping) you may have on hand along with leftover meat such as the Mini Meatballs (page 217). Feel free to use more leftover soup if you have it—is there such a thing as too many caramelized onions?

**1.** Preheat the oven to 350°F [180°C] and grease a 9 by 13 in [23 by 33 cm] baking dish.

**2.** Place a fine-mesh strainer over a medium bowl and pour in the soup. Leave the solids from the soup in the strainer and measure out 1½ cups [360 ml] of broth from the soup for the recipe (add additional vegetable broth or water if it comes out to less than 1½ cups [360 ml]). Discard the remaining broth or save for another use.

**3.** Arrange the bread in a single layer on a baking sheet and bake for 8 minutes, or until starting to get toasty and dried out. Transfer to the prepared baking dish and spread into an even layer.

**4.** Whisk the leftover caramelized onions from the soup back into the broth, along with the milk, eggs, mustard, thyme, salt, and half of the Gruyère. Pour the mixture evenly over the bread and top with the remaining cheese and a few grinds of pepper.

**5.** Bake for 35 to 40 minutes, or until the filling is cooked all the way through (it shouldn't jiggle very much) and the top has started to brown. Serve warm. To store, let cool completely, cover in aluminum foil, and keep in the fridge for up to 2 days.

# Broccoli-Cheddar Soup

Serves 4 to 6

4 Tbsp [55 g] unsalted butter

1 white onion, diced

2 celery stalks, diced

1 tsp salt

2 garlic cloves, minced

2 tsp ground mustard

½ tsp freshly ground black pepper

¼ tsp cayenne pepper

¼ cup [35 g] all-purpose flour

4 cups [960 ml] Homemade Roasted Vegetable Broth (page 209) or store-bought low-sodium vegetable broth

1 lb [455 g] broccoli florets, chopped (about 4 cups)

2 carrots, peeled and cut into matchsticks

8 oz [230 g] sharp Cheddar cheese, shredded

4 oz [115 g] medium Cheddar cheese, shredded

1 cup [240 ml] half-and-half

Pinch of grated nutmeg (optional)

**Meat Suggestion**

Crumble some Candied Bacon (page 216) over the soup when serving.

I wanted the recipes in this book to feel like a mix of both familiar and new. This recipe falls strictly into the familiar camp, as I tried to make it taste as much like the broccoli-Cheddar soup you might have had at your favorite lunch soup spot. If you like your soup thick and rich, like the popular version served at Panera Bread, you can reduce the vegetable broth to 3 cups [720 ml] and up the half-and-half to 2 cups [480 ml].

1. In a Dutch oven or large stockpot over medium heat, melt the butter. Add the onion, celery, and ½ tsp of the salt and cook until softened and tender, about 5 minutes. Add the garlic, mustard, black pepper, and cayenne and sauté for another 30 seconds. Add the flour and whisk until it starts to turn golden, 2 to 3 minutes. Add the vegetable broth, broccoli, carrots, and remaining ½ tsp of salt. Increase the heat to high and bring to a boil.

2. Turn down the heat to medium-low and simmer until the broccoli is cooked through, 15 to 20 minutes. Add both Cheddar cheeses and the half-and-half and stir until the cheese is completely melted, 1 minute. Taste and season with a pinch of nutmeg (if using) and salt and pepper as needed. Serve warm.

☞ **Storing:** Store leftovers refrigerated in an airtight container for up to 2 days. I do not recommend freezing this due to all the dairy.

**Quick Fix**
Serve topped with Fennel-Rye Croutons (page 215) for extra crunch.

# Baked Broccoli-Cheddar Pasta

### Serves 4

9 oz [255 g] medium pasta shells (about 3 cups)

1 Tbsp unsalted butter

½ cup [30 g] panko bread crumbs

1 garlic clove, minced

4 cups [960 ml] Broccoli-Cheddar Soup (page 111)

4 oz [115 g] medium Cheddar cheese, shredded

Although it seems unlikely that you won't want to enjoy the Broccoli-Cheddar Soup leftovers as they are, I am giving you an equally comforting repurpose option in the form of this cheesy baked pasta dish. Use the time it takes in the oven to whip up one of the salads toward the back of the book as a side. I suggest the Italian-ish Chopped Salad (page 221) or the Brussels Sprouts Salad (page 229).

1. Preheat the oven to 350°F [180°C] and grease a 9 in [23 cm] square baking dish. Bring a large pot of salted water to a boil over high heat. Add the pasta and cook until al dente, about 9 minutes or according to the package directions. Drain, reserving 1 cup [240 ml] of the pasta cooking water.

2. In a small skillet over medium heat, melt the butter. Add the bread crumbs and garlic and sauté until the bread crumbs have browned, 3 to 4 minutes. Transfer to a small bowl.

3. In a large bowl, stir together the cooked pasta, soup, three-quarters of the cheese, and the reserved cooking water. Pour into the prepared baking dish and top with remaining cheese and bread crumbs.

4. Bake for 20 minutes, or until heated through and starting to bubble around the edges. Serve warm. Store leftovers in an airtight container in the fridge for up to 2 days.

### Quick Fix

If you are not from the Midwest, then you have probably never experienced Cincinnati Skyline Chili and all this is going to sound a bit goofy, but stay with me. Enjoy your chili three-way, which in Cincinnati means over spaghetti and topped with a mound of cheese. Since we are doing this with bean chili instead of beef, it may not be authentic, but it is absolutely delicious. Cook 8 oz [230 g] spaghetti according to the package directions and drain. Transfer to a serving dish and top with 2 cups [480 ml] leftover chili and then 2 oz [55 g] (or more if you like it extra cheesy!) shredded Cheddar cheese. If you want to bulk it up even more, you can add finely diced onions to make it a four-way chili!

# Chipotle Cocoa Three-Bean Chili

Serves 6 to 8

¼ cup [60 ml] olive oil

1 red onion, diced

1 yellow or orange bell pepper, diced

3 garlic cloves, minced

1 chipotle in adobo sauce (2 if you like a lot of spice), chopped

2 Tbsp chili powder

1 Tbsp cocoa powder

½ Tbsp brown sugar

½ Tbsp smoked paprika

½ Tbsp ground cumin

1 tsp dried oregano

1 tsp salt

2½ cups [600 ml] Homemade Roasted Vegetable Broth (page 209) or store-bought low-sodium vegetable broth

One 14 oz [400 g] can black beans, rinsed

One 14 oz [400 g] can kidney beans, rinsed

One 14 oz [400 g] can pinto beans, rinsed

One 14½ oz [415 g] can fire-roasted diced tomatoes

One 4 oz [115 g] can diced green chiles

1 Tbsp fresh lime juice

### Topping Options

Sour cream

Shredded Cheddar cheese

Fresh cilantro leaves

Avocado slices

Halved cherry tomatoes

Sliced green onions

Fritos

Tortilla chips

### Meat Suggestion

Add crumbled Candied Bacon (page 216) to the array of toppings you serve this with.

To me, a robust bean chili is kind of the perfect soup. It is filling and flavorful and can easily feed a crowd without breaking the bank. I make this chili recipe often when having friends over because it's not only inexpensive and delicious but also works with lots of different diet preferences (vegetarian, vegan, gluten-free) so I don't have to worry about making different versions for everyone. I always put out a variety of toppings so my guests can customize to their liking. Don't be intimidated by the long ingredient list! There is a good chance you probably already have most of the ingredients on hand to make this.

1. In a large saucepan or Dutch oven over medium heat, warm the oil. Add the red onion and bell pepper and sauté until soft, about 7 minutes. Add the garlic, chipotle, chili powder, cocoa powder, brown sugar, paprika, cumin, oregano, and salt and sauté until the spices are fragrant and have coated the vegetables, 30 seconds.

2. Pour in the vegetable broth, black beans, kidney beans, pinto beans, tomatoes with their juice, and green chiles. Turn the heat to medium-high and bring to a boil. Lower the heat to medium-low, cover, and simmer for at least 20 minutes. Remove the lid and simmer until the chili thickens and it's reached your desired consistency, 10 to 15 minutes more (note that it will thicken up more as it cools as well).

3. Remove from the heat and stir in the lime juice. Taste and season with salt and pepper as needed. Ladle into bowls, add toppings (if using), and serve.

☞ **Slow Cooker:** Sauté the onions, peppers, and spices as in step 1. Add the tomatoes and their juice to deglaze the pan. Transfer to a slow cooker along with the vegetable broth, black beans, kidney beans, pinto beans, and green chiles. Cover and cook for 4 hours on high. Continue with the recipe from step 3.

☞ **Storing:** Store leftovers refrigerated in an airtight container for up to 3 days or freeze for up to 3 months.

# Cheesy Bean & Roasted Red Pepper Empanadas

### Makes 18 empanadas

### Dough

4½ cups [630 g] all-purpose flour

2 Tbsp sugar

½ tsp salt

1¼ cups [275 g] unsalted butter or vegetable shortening, cut into small cubes

8 oz [240 ml] light beer

1 egg, lightly beaten with 1 tsp water

### Filing

2 cups [480 ml] Chipotle Cocoa Three-Bean Chili (page 117), drained

½ cup [125 g] chopped roasted red peppers

2 oz [55 g] Cheddar cheese, shredded

### Cilantro-Lime Topping

2 Tbsp finely chopped fresh cilantro

1 Tbsp olive oil

1 Tbsp fresh lime juice

Pinch of salt

With most of my stepmom's relatives living across the country or across the border, I've always appreciated the way she's tried to connect us to them through food. Holidays were spent helping her fill tamales and empanadas made from recipes passed down for generations. Although I tended to gravitate toward the sweet empanadas she'd fill with apple or pumpkin when I was a kid, I played around with these savory ones for the book and loved them.

Before asking her for the recipe, I tried to tackle developing this myself and repeatedly ended up with dry dough that would fall apart when baked. Finally I asked how she made her dough so soft to the touch when rolling but flaky once baked, and she told me carbonation was the answer. What carbonated liquid was actually used in the original recipe she was taught decades ago is unclear, but through trial and error she has found that Sprite in sweet dough and light beer in savory is the way to go. Just as she always puts her own spin on it and tries out new fillings each year, I'm happy to present this cheesy bean chili version I crafted just for you all.

1. **Make the dough:** In a large bowl, whisk together the flour, sugar, and salt. Use clean hands to work the butter into the dough until only pea-size pieces remain. Make a well in the center of the dough and slowly pour in the beer while mixing, just until completely combined and no longer dry. Cover and set aside to rest.

2. **Make the filling:** In a medium bowl, stir together the chili, red peppers, and Cheddar. Cover and refrigerate until ready to use.

3. Preheat the oven to 400°F [200°C] and line two baking sheets with parchment paper. Measure out 1 oz [30 g] of dough and roll into a ball. Repeat with the rest of the dough (you should end up with sixteen balls). On a lightly floured surface, roll out a dough ball to a 4 in [10 cm] circle. Sprinkle a pinch of flour on the middle of the dough and top with 2 Tbsp of filling. Brush the edges of the dough with the egg wash. Fold the circle over the filling to create a half-moon shape and press around the edges with your fingers to seal. Transfer to a prepared baking sheet and crimp the edges by pressing down around them with a fork. Repeat rolling out, filling, and sealing with the remaining dough and filling. Space the empanadas at least 2 in [5 cm] apart on the baking sheet.

4. Brush the tops of the empanadas with the remaining egg wash and cut a small slit in the top of each to allow steam to escape. Bake for 18 to 20 minutes or until golden on top.

5. **Meanwhile, make the cilantro-lime topping:** In a small bowl, whisk together the cilantro, oil, lime juice, and a pinch of salt. Serve the empanadas warm, with the cilantro-lime mixture on top.

Quick Fix: Cincinnati Chili p. 116

# Soup Swap

Every winter a group of friends and I come together for a soup swap. Someone volunteers their house to host and we each come with a big pot of soup, a side (usually bread, a salad, or an appetizer we can munch on while mingling), and lots of leftovers containers. We then spend an hour or so catching up and sampling the soups. When it's time to go, we all fill up our soup containers with whichever soups we preferred so we'll then have a fridge or freezer full of soups to enjoy for later. Not only is this a fun social event, but I also love trying new soups I wouldn't have thought of making.

Alternatively, you could also start a monthly "soup group" where you rotate going to each other's houses, and the host prepares a simple meal of a soup and a side or two. (No need to get fancy with table settings or anything like that!) This takes the pressure off you to cook for each other every month and gives you an excuse to meet over a delicious meal. A lot of the recipes in the book are perfect for this, as they allow you to prepare the soup for many different types of diets. For example, I usually recommend adding the meat or pasta in at the end of a recipe. When cooking for company, leave those things on the side for guests to add if they'd like.

# Cream of Asparagus

3 Tbsp unsalted butter

2 shallots, diced

2 lb [910 g] asparagus, trimmed and cut into 1½ in [4 cm] pieces

½ tsp fresh thyme, plus more for serving

½ tsp salt

¼ tsp freshly ground black pepper

4 cups [960 ml] Homemade Roasted Vegetable Broth (page 209) or store-bought low-sodium vegetable broth

½ cup [120 g] crème fraîche, plus more for serving

1 tsp fresh lemon juice

Olive oil, for serving

## Meat Suggestion

You can add crumbled Candied Bacon (page 216) when serving but be careful to not overdo it—the bacon can quickly overpower the delicate flavor of this soup.

## Quick Fix

Serve reheated soup with Fennel-Rye Croutons (page 215).

This delicate soup is a wonderful addition to a spring gathering alongside an egg dish and a vinegary salad (perhaps the Mostly Vegetables Potato Salad recipe on page 152?). The ingredient list is simple, as I selected elements that would enhance but not overpower the subtle asparagus flavor. I recommend using green asparagus, as the purple asparagus can turn a slightly unappealing gray color when blended.

1. In a Dutch oven over medium heat, melt 2 Tbsp of the butter. Add the shallots and cook until softened, 2 to 3 minutes. Add the asparagus, thyme, salt, and pepper and sauté until the asparagus has softened, about 7 minutes.

2. Add the vegetable broth and 1 cup [240 ml] of water and bring to a boil over high heat. Turn the heat down to medium-low and simmer until the asparagus is tender and easily pierced with a fork, 15 to 20 minutes.

3. Remove from the heat and use an immersion blender to blend until smooth. Whisk in the crème fraîche, lemon juice, and the remaining 1 Tbsp of butter. Taste and season with salt and lemon juice as needed.

4. Divide among serving bowls and finish with a drizzle of oil, a dollop of crème fraîche, and a sprinkle of thyme.

☞ **Pressure Cooker:** Use the sauté function on your pressure cooker to cook the shallot and asparagus as in step 1. Turn the sauté function off and add the vegetable broth (no need to add the water). Pressure cook on high for 5 minutes, then quick release. Continue with the recipe from step 3.

☞ **Storing:** Store leftovers refrigerated in an airtight container for up to 3 days. I do not recommend freezing due to the dairy.

# Savory Asparagus Dutch Baby

**Serves 4**

3 Tbsp unsalted butter

½ cup [120 ml] Cream of Asparagus (page 127)

¼ cup [60 ml] whole milk

3 eggs, at room temperature

¾ cup [105 g] all-purpose flour

1 tsp sugar

¼ tsp salt

With its dramatic presentation, a Dutch baby feels like such a statement when serving it at your breakfast table. For the best rise, it's important that the ingredients are at room temperature before you start cooking. If your eggs are still cold, place them in a small bowl with lukewarm water for a few minutes to bring them to room temperature quickly.

The options are endless when it comes to topping this savory Dutch baby. I recommend some sautéed asparagus (for example, if you have some left over from the soup you made yesterday), poached or scrambled eggs, and a blender hollandaise or Citrus-Artichoke White Pesto (page 214). Meat-eaters may like it with some crumbled Candied Bacon (page 216), or keep it simple with just a few pats of herby compound butter.

**1.** Preheat the oven to 425°F [220°C] and place a 10 in [25 cm] ovenproof skillet in the oven to heat up.

**2.** Place 2 Tbsp of the butter in a small heatproof bowl and microwave for 15 to 20 seconds, or until melted. Transfer to a high-speed blender and allow it to cool to room temperature. Pour the soup and milk into the same small bowl (no need to clean it) and microwave for 30 seconds to take the chill off and transfer to the blender. Add the eggs, flour, sugar, and salt to the blender and blend until completely mixed, about 30 seconds.

**3.** Carefully, using a potholder, remove the hot skillet from the oven and add the remaining 1 Tbsp of butter. Swirl the pan around to coat with the butter and pour in the batter. Transfer back to the oven and bake for 12 to 15 minutes, or until golden and puffed.

**4.** Use a spatula to transfer the Dutch baby to a cutting board and slice into quarters. Serve warm, with whatever toppings you are craving.

# Red Cabbage Soup with Crème Fraîche & Dill

**Serves 6**

1 Tbsp unsalted butter

1 Tbsp olive oil

1 red onion, diced

2 garlic cloves, minced

½ Tbsp caraway seeds

8 cups chopped red cabbage (from 1 head, about 2½ lb [1.1 kg])

1 Yukon gold potato, peeled and diced

1 tsp salt

4 cups [960 ml] Homemade Roasted Vegetable Broth (page 209) or store-bought low-sodium vegetable broth

½ tsp freshly ground black pepper

1 Tbsp apple cider vinegar

4 oz [115 g] crème fraîche, plus more for serving

Dill sprigs, for serving

**Meat Suggestion**

Because this soup is so silky, I love to pile on the toppings to give it a bit of textural variety. Crumbled Candied Bacon (page 216) is a delicious addition.

**Quick Fix**

Whip up a batch of Fennel Rye Croutons (page 215) to add a crunchy topping to this silky soup.

I'm not a fan of the flavor of beets, which as a food photographer is very frustrating because they make beautiful and vibrant dishes. Because of this, I was legitimately giddy when I came across a beautiful purple soup made with red cabbage. (A purple soup made without beets? How did I get so lucky?). Although it's not clear if this soup was originally from Eastern Europe or Russia, I've tweaked it so much that it's now very far from the original. The addition of potato makes it extra creamy, crème fraîche adds richness, and apple cider vinegar brings balance. If you can't find crème fraîche in your market, you can substitute sour cream or mascarpone.

1. In a Dutch oven over medium heat, melt the butter and warm the oil. Add the onion and sauté until softened, 5 to 7 minutes. Add the garlic and caraway seeds and sauté until fragrant, 30 seconds. Set aside ½ cup [30 g] of the cabbage for topping. Add the remaining cabbage, potato, and salt and sauté until the cabbage has softened, about 5 minutes.

2. Add the vegetable broth, 2 cups [480 ml] of water, and the pepper, and bring to a boil over high heat. Turn the heat down to medium-low and simmer for at least 20 minutes to develop flavor.

3. Remove from the heat and stir in the vinegar. Use an immersion blender to blend until completely smooth. Stir in the crème fraîche. Taste and season with salt and pepper as needed. Serve topped with the reserved cabbage, more crème fraîche, and a sprinkle of dill.

☞ **Pressure Cooker:** Use the sauté function to cook the vegetables as in step 1. Add the vegetable broth, 1½ cups [360 ml] of water (instead of 2 cups [480 ml]), and the pepper. Pressure cook on high for 7 minutes, then quick release. Continue with the recipe from step 3.

☞ **Storing:** Store leftovers refrigerated in an airtight container for up to 3 days. If you are wanting to freeze, do not add the crème fraîche. Freeze in an airtight container for up to 2 months. Make a note on the container to add crème fraîche, and how much. (If you freeze half the soup, for example, note that you should add 2 oz [55 g] crème fraîche after reheating.)

# Bibb Salad with Rye Croutons, Dried Apricots & Dill

**Serves 4**

### Dressing

¼ cup [60 ml] Red Cabbage Soup (page 131)

1 Tbsp red wine vinegar

1 tsp Dijon mustard

1 tsp honey

½ tsp salt

¼ tsp freshly ground black pepper

3 Tbsp olive oil

### Salad

2 heads Bibb lettuce, trimmed, leaves washed and torn into bite-size pieces

4 oz [115 g] white Cheddar or provolone cheese, cubed

1 cup [40 g] Fennel-Rye Croutons (page 215)

7 dried apricots [55 g], quartered

2 Tbsp chopped fresh dill

I love that this salad uses a lot of the same ingredients as the Red Cabbage Soup (page 131), so if you made that yesterday, you probably already have them on hand. I like to keep the ingredient list short when it comes to Bibb salads since it's so easy to weigh down this light lettuce. It's also important to not dress this salad until right before serving and start by adding only half the dressing. I like to serve the remainder on the side so that diners may choose how much dressing they want.

1. **Make the dressing:** In a small bowl, whisk together the soup, vinegar, mustard, honey, salt, and pepper. Slowly pour in oil while whisking to emulsify. Taste and season with salt and pepper as needed.

2. **Make the salad:** Arrange the Bibb leaves on a serving platter. Scatter over the cheese, croutons, and apricots. When ready to serve, drizzle half the dressing over the salad and top with the dill. Serve the remaining dressing on the side.

# Pressure Cooker Black Bean Soup with Orange & Cumin

**Serves 8 to 10**

1 Tbsp olive oil

1 red onion, diced

1 lb [455 g] black beans, soaked overnight and drained

1 navel orange, quartered

1 red, yellow, or orange bell pepper, quartered

8 garlic cloves, smashed

1 chipotle in adobo sauce, plus 1 Tbsp sauce (add an extra chipotle if you like a lot of spice)

1 strip kombu (optional)

2 bay leaves

2 tsp salt

2 tsp ground cumin

1 tsp smoked paprika

4 cups [960 ml] Homemade Roasted Vegetable Broth (page 209) or store-bought low-sodium vegetable broth

1 tsp red wine vinegar

### Topping Options

Frizzled Shallots (page 211)

Chopped fresh cilantro

Shredded Cheddar cheese

Tortilla chips or Fritos

### Meat Suggestion

Add Spicy Shrimp (page 216) to the toppings.

### Quick Fix

Add freshness to your leftover soup by topping it with a simple salsa: Toss together 1 pint [320 g] quartered cherry tomatoes, ¼ cup [35 g] finely diced red onion, 1 diced small jalapeño (keep the seeds if you like spice), 2 Tbsp chopped fresh cilantro, 1 Tbsp fresh lime juice, and ¼ tsp salt. Taste and season with salt and lime juice as needed.

There is nothing I love making in a pressure cooker more than dried beans. The pressure allows the beans to absorb flavor in a fraction of the time it takes on the stovetop and the end result is always silky and delicious. I prefer using Rancho Gordo's Midnight Black Beans in this recipe, but other bean brands will do in a pinch.

This recipe is inspired by Joe Yonan's recipe for Cuban-style orange-scented black beans, which I always turn to when I need to make a batch of beans for enchiladas or burrito bowls. While preserving the technique and flavors, I've adapted the recipe slightly to turn it into a puréed soup recipe. If you have kombu on hand, feel free to throw in a sheet, as it's been said to aid in the digestion of beans without altering the flavor.

1. In the pressure cooker on the sauté setting, heat the oil. Add the onion and sauté until softened, 3 to 5 minutes. Turn the pressure cooker off and add the beans, orange quarters, bell pepper, garlic, chipotle, adobo sauce, kombu (if using), bay leaves, salt, cumin, paprika, vegetable broth, and 4 cups [960 ml] of water and stir to combine. Pressure cook on high for 45 minutes. Allow the pressure to release naturally, then remove the lid to release any excess steam.

2. Remove 1½ cups [360 ml] of liquid from the top and discard. Use a fork to fish out the kombu (if it hasn't fallen apart), bay leaves, and orange quarters (which should mostly just be the peel at this point) and remove. Use an immersion blender to blend the soup until smooth. Once cool enough to taste, stir in the vinegar and season with salt and pepper as needed.

3. Serve with the toppings of your choice.

☞ **Storing:** Store leftovers refrigerated in an airtight container for up to 3 days or freeze for up to 3 months.

# Stuffed Poblano Peppers

**Serves 4**

1 Tbsp unsalted butter

1 cup [200 g] long-grain white rice

1 tsp garlic powder

½ tsp ground cumin

½ tsp onion powder

¼ tsp salt

2 cups [480 ml] Homemade Roasted Vegetable Broth (page 209) or store-bought low-sodium vegetable broth

8 oz [240 ml] red enchilada sauce

4 large poblano peppers

1⅓ cups [320 ml] Pressure Cooker Black Bean Soup with Orange & Cumin (page 135)

2 cups [40 g] baby spinach

4 oz [115 g] cherry tomatoes, quartered

4 oz [115 g] pepper Jack cheese, shredded

Fresh cilantro leaves, for serving (optional)

For these stuffed poblanos, seek out the biggest peppers you can find. When cutting them open from end to end, make sure to create an opening big enough so that they can be stuffed without the filling running out. I love to serve this as an easy weeknight vegetarian main dish with a side salad (such as the Kale Salad with Parsley-Lemon Vinaigrette on page 223).

**1.** In a medium saucepan over medium heat, melt the butter. Add the rice and sauté until toasted, about 5 minutes. Add the garlic powder, cumin, onion power, and salt and sauté until fragrant, 30 seconds. Add the vegetable broth and ½ cup [120 ml] of the enchilada sauce. Bring to a boil, then cover, lower the heat to low, and cook until the rice is tender, 15 to 20 minutes. Remove from the heat and set aside, covered, to rest for at least 5 minutes before using.

**2.** Preheat the oven to 400°F [200°C]. Cut a lengthwise hole out of the side of each of the poblanos and remove the seeds. Arrange the peppers, cut-sides up, in an 8 in [20 cm] square baking dish in a single layer.

**3.** Spoon ⅓ cup [80 ml] of the soup into each poblano. Fluff the rice with a fork and fold in the spinach and cherry tomatoes. Divide the rice among the poblanos, filling any leftover room in the inside of the poblanos and creating big mounds of rice over the top. Drizzle the remaining enchilada sauce over the stuffed peppers and then sprinkle them with the cheese.

**4.** Bake for 20 to 25 minutes, or until the cheese is melted and browned. Sprinkle with a few cilantro leaves, if desired, and serve. Store leftovers in an airtight container in the fridge for up to 2 days.

Pressure Cooker Black Bean Soup with Orange & Cumin

# Caramelized Spring Onion Ramen

**Serves 4**

¼ cup [60 ml] olive oil or canola oil

4 bunches spring onions (13 oz [370 g] total), thinly sliced (about 4 cups)

½ tsp salt

2 in [5 cm] piece fresh ginger, peeled and grated

3 garlic cloves, minced

1 Tbsp miso paste

1 tsp chili-garlic sauce

½ tsp ground turmeric

¼ tsp freshly ground black pepper

4 cups [960 ml] Homemade Roasted Vegetable Broth (page 209) or store-bought low-sodium vegetable broth

½ Tbsp tamari or low-sodium soy sauce

3 packages ramen noodles, flavor packets discarded

1 baby bok choy, trimmed and quartered

1 carrot, peeled and cut into matchsticks

1 cup [100 g] snow peas

1 tsp rice vinegar

Fresh cilantro leaves, sesame oil, and chili oil or hot sauce, for serving (optional)

**Meat Suggestion**

Topping each bowl with a few pieces of Spicy Shrimp (page 216) is a light addition that won't overwhelm the delicate spring onions.

**Quick Fix**

Poach or soft-boil an egg (1 for each serving) to top your bowl of ramen.

Making your own flavored broth instead of relying on ramen seasoning packets is an easy and affordable way to turn this low-budget staple into a hearty meal. Caramelizing the spring onions brings sweetness to the dish while tamari packs the salty punch and crisp vegetables fill it out. We add the vegetables just at the very end so they absorb some of the flavor from the broth while still staying crunchy and bright.

**1.** In a large Dutch oven or stockpot over medium-low heat, warm the oil. Add the onions and salt and cook until very soft and just starting to brown in some parts, 12 to 15 minutes. Add the ginger and garlic and sauté until fragrant, 30 seconds. Stir in the miso, chili-garlic sauce, turmeric, and pepper and cook for an additional 30 seconds or until fragrant. Add the vegetable broth, tamari, and 2 cups [480 ml] of water and bring to a boil over high heat. Lower the heat to medium-low and simmer for 10 minutes to develop the flavor.

**2.** Meanwhile, bring a large pot of water to a boil over high heat. Add the noodles and cook for 3 minutes. Drain.

**3.** Add the bok choy, carrot, and snow peas to the simmering broth and cook just until the vegetables are starting to soften, 2 minutes. Remove from the heat and stir in the vinegar. Taste and season with more vinegar, tamari (for salt), and chili-garlic sauce (for spice) as needed.

**4.** Divide the noodles among four bowls and ladle the broth and veggies over the noodles. Top with cilantro and sprinkles of sesame oil and chili oil.

☞ **Storing:** Store leftover soup and noodles refrigerated in separate airtight containers for up to 2 days. If you want to freeze it, remove the noodles and freeze the broth with the veggies for up to 2 months.

# Smoky French Lentil Soup with White Balsamic Reduction

**Serves 8**

1 Tbsp olive oil

1 yellow onion, diced

2 celery stalks, diced

2 carrots, peeled and diced

3 garlic cloves, minced

3 thyme sprigs, plus more for serving

1 Tbsp smoked paprika

1 tsp salt

⅛ tsp cayenne pepper

4 cups [960 ml] Homemade Roasted Vegetable Broth (page 209) or store-bought low-sodium vegetable broth

One 14½ oz [415 g] can diced fire-roasted tomatoes

1 cup [200 g] French green lentils, rinsed

2 bay leaves

½ cup [120 ml] white balsamic vinegar

1 Tbsp red wine vinegar

### Meat Suggestion

Add extra flavor by topping this soup with crumbled Candied Bacon (page 216).

### Quick Fix

When reheating the soup, stir in a handful of your favorite greens, such as baby spinach, baby kale, or arugula (stemmed and chopped into bite-size pieces if large).

This is one of my favorite soups to turn to when I'm craving something nutritious and simple. I love the way French lentils hold their shape a bit better than other lentil varieties, so make sure you are using them in this recipe.

**1.** In a large Dutch oven over medium heat, warm the oil. Add the onion, celery, and carrots and sauté until softened, 5 to 7 minutes. Add the garlic, thyme, paprika, salt, and cayenne and sauté until fragrant, 30 seconds.

**2.** Add the vegetable broth, 2 cups [480 ml] of water, the tomatoes and their juice, lentils, and bay leaves and bring to a boil over high heat. Lower the heat to medium-low and simmer until the lentils are tender but still holding their shape, 25 to 30 minutes.

**3.** Meanwhile, add the white balsamic vinegar to a small skillet or saucepan and simmer over medium heat until reduced by half, 5 to 7 minutes. Set aside.

**4.** Remove the soup from the heat and stir in the red wine vinegar. Remove the thyme sprigs, taste, and season with salt and pepper as needed. Serve the white balsamic reduction alongside the soup so people can drizzle some into their bowls.

☞ **Pressure Cooker:** Use the sauté function on your pressure cooker to sauté the aromatics as in step 1. Turn the sauté function off, add the vegetable broth, 1 cup [240 ml] of water (down from 2 cups [480 ml]), the tomatoes, lentils, and bay leaves, and stir to combine. Pressure cook on high for 15 minutes, then quick release. Continue with the recipe from step 3.

☞ **Storing:** Store leftover soup refrigerated in an airtight container for up to 4 days or freeze for up to 3 months. Store leftover reduced balsamic vinegar in an airtight container in the fridge for up to 2 weeks.

# Rice & Lentil Pilaf with Pickled Raisins & Pistachios

**Serves 2 as a main
or 4 as a side**

2 Tbsp ghee or unsalted butter

2 yellow onions, sliced

1 cup [200 g] basmati rice

2 garlic cloves, minced

½ Tbsp garam masala

½ tsp ground cinnamon

½ tsp ground turmeric

½ tsp salt

1½ cups [360 ml] Homemade
Roasted Vegetable Broth
(page 209) or store-bought low-
sodium vegetable broth

⅓ cup [45 g] golden raisins

2 Tbsp rice vinegar

⅔ cup [160 ml] Smoky French
Lentil Soup (page 143), drained

2 Tbsp chopped fresh cilantro,
plus more for serving

Freshly ground black pepper,
to taste

⅓ cup [45 g] roasted pistachios

With biryani being my go-to meal at our favorite Indian restaurant, I've come to realize I love hearty rice dishes as a main. This one is particularly addictive thanks to the mix of savory spices, sweet quick-pickled raisins, and salty pistachios. Wyatt wants you to know that you could also fold some Shredded Chicken (page 217) into this dish as well, if you'd like.

1. In a medium saucepan over medium-low heat, melt the ghee. Add the onions and cook until very soft but not browning, 18 to 20 minutes. Add the rice, garlic, garam masala, cinnamon, turmeric, and salt and sauté until fragrant, 1 to 2 minutes. Stir in the vegetable broth and bring to a boil over high heat. Cover, lower the heat to medium-low, and simmer until the rice is tender, 10 to 12 minutes. Remove from the heat but keep covered and set aside to steam for 10 minutes.

2. Meanwhile, combine the raisins and vinegar in a small bowl and add enough water just to cover the raisins. Set aside to lightly pickle while the rice cooks.

3. In a large skillet, cook the soup until very hot (165°F [75°C]) and most of the moisture has cooked off, 3 to 5 minutes. Remove from the heat, add the rice and cilantro, and stir to combine. Taste and season with salt and pepper as needed. Drain the raisins.

4. Transfer the pilaf to a serving platter and top with the raisins, pistachios, and more cilantro. Serve right away.

# Confit Shallots with Lentils & Lemon

**Serves 6 as a side**

1½ lb [680 g] shallots and/or pearl onions, peeled, trimmed, and cut to a consistent size

5 garlic cloves, lightly crushed

10 thyme sprigs

1 lemon, quartered and seeds removed

½ tsp salt

½ cup [120 ml] olive oil

2 cups [480 ml] Smoky French Lentil Soup (page 143)

Parsley or dill sprigs and crème fraîche (optional but delightful), for serving

This recipe is not for the impatient. Peeling a large amount of shallots is no quick task (in reality, it takes 10 minutes or so but it feels like a rather long time when you are in it). But if you have the time and patience, this dish is wonderful. The onions slow-cook in olive oil, lemon, and thyme and then are spooned over your leftover lentils for a stunning side dish.

The onions won't be completely submerged in the oil at first (which is unusual when confitting), but they cook down as they bake and will eventually be completely covered. Olive oil is expensive, so I tried to make sure you use only what is absolutely necessary. I like to use a mix of shallots and pearl onions for this recipe, but including both in the title was just way too lengthy. You want them all to be about the same size, so go ahead and halve or even quarter some of the shallots if they are larger than others.

1. Preheat the oven to 350°F [180°C]. Add the onions, garlic, thyme, lemon wedges, and salt to a small baking dish. Pour the oil over the top and cover the dish with foil. Bake for 1 hour, stirring halfway through.

2. Meanwhile, reheat the soup in a small saucepan over medium heat until heated through (at least 165°F [75°C]). Drain the excess liquid and transfer the lentils to a serving dish.

3. Remove the shallots from the oven, uncover, and discard the thyme. Squeeze the juice from the lemon wedges over the shallots and discard the lemon rinds. Use a slotted spoon to scoop the onions over the lentils. Sprinkle with a few sprigs of parsley or dill and serve with crème fraîche, if desired, on the side.

# Spring Vegetable Chowder

**Serves 8 to 10**

3 Tbsp unsalted butter

1 bunch spring onions or green onions, trimmed and sliced

1½ lb [680 g] new potatoes, cut into ½ in [13 mm] pieces

1 bunch asparagus (about 8 oz [230 g]), trimmed and cut into 1 in [2.5 cm] pieces

1 tsp fresh thyme leaves

3 garlic cloves, minced

⅓ cup [45 g] all-purpose flour

4 cups [960 ml] Homemade Roasted Vegetable Broth (page 209) or store-bought low-sodium vegetable broth

1 tsp salt

¼ tsp freshly ground black pepper

1 cup [120 g] peas (fresh or frozen)

1 cup [240 ml] whole milk or half-and-half

¼ cup [10 g] chopped fresh dill, plus more for serving

1 Tbsp fresh lemon juice

1 radish, thinly sliced, for serving (optional)

**Meat Suggestion**

Topping with some crumbled Candied Bacon (page 216) instead of radishes would pair delightfully with the potatoes in the chowder.

**Quick Fix**

Add some store-bought or homemade gnocchi to your chowder when reheating it (the Ricotta Gnocchi on page 40 without the tomato sauce would be fantastic). Note that you may need to add some additional broth to the chowder when reheating, as it may have thickened up in the fridge.

I tend to go a little overboard at the farmers' market when spring produce starts to pop up. I can't help myself—it's just so exciting to see something besides root vegetables and winter squash in the stalls. I developed this chowder for those damp spring days when you are still craving something hearty but want to use your spring market haul. This soup is very forgiving, so feel free to use whatever kind of potatoes you have on hand, swap spring onions for ramps or green onions, and use fresh or frozen peas.

1. In a large Dutch oven or stockpot over medium heat, melt the butter. Add the onions, potatoes, and asparagus and sauté until starting to soften, 5 to 7 minutes. Add the thyme leaves and garlic and sauté until fragrant, 30 seconds. Add the flour and sauté until starting to gain color, 2 to 3 minutes.

2. Add the vegetable broth, 1 cup [240 ml] of water, the salt, and pepper and bring to a boil over high heat. Turn the heat down to medium-low and simmer until the potatoes are easily pierced with a fork, about 10 minutes. Add the peas and simmer just until the peas are cooked all the way through, about 5 minutes. Use the back of a wooden spoon to slightly smash a few of the potatoes so they release their starches.

3. Remove from the heat and add the milk, dill, and lemon juice. Taste and season with salt, pepper, and lemon juice as needed. Serve warm, topped with radish slices, if desired, and more dill.

☞ **Storing:** Store leftovers refrigerated in an airtight container for up to 3 days. I do not recommend freezing this soup due to the dairy.

# Mostly Vegetables Potato Salad

**Serves 8 to 10 as a side**

⅓ cup [80 ml] olive oil

¼ cup [60 ml] white wine vinegar or red wine vinegar

¼ cup [10 g] chopped fresh dill, parsley, tarragon, chives, or a mix of all

1 Tbsp whole-grain mustard

1 tsp sugar or honey

½ tsp salt

½ tsp freshly ground black pepper

4 green onions, thinly sliced

3 celery stalks, diced

3 cups [720 ml] Spring Vegetable Chowder (page 151)

4 eggs

Can you tell I didn't know what to name this recipe? It's made in the same way you'd make a vinaigrette-based potato salad, but while traditional potato salads are mostly just potatoes (obviously), this salad is more vegetable-heavy while still being prepared in the same way as a potato salad.

The tangy vinaigrette brings freshness to the leftover vegetables while the celery adds new crunch and jammy eggs fill it all out. I like to reheat the chowder in its liquid to get the vegetables warmed up before straining and tossing the chowder vegetables with the rest of the salad. You can then serve the salad slightly warm or cover and chill for a few hours to give it more time for the flavors to meld.

**1.** In a large bowl, whisk together the oil, vinegar, herbs, mustard, sugar, salt, and pepper. Add the green onions and celery and toss to coat. Set aside.

**2.** In a medium saucepan, combine the chowder with 1 cup [240 ml] of water to thin it out. Heat over medium heat until simmering and warmed through. Remove from the heat and drain. Transfer the solids to the bowl with the dressing and toss to coat.

**3.** Place the eggs in a small saucepan and add enough water to cover. Bring to a boil over high heat, then lower the heat and simmer for 5 minutes. Drain and rinse under cold water for 1 minute. As soon as they are cool enough to handle, peel them and cut into quarters. Add to the salad and toss to coat.

**4.** Taste and season with salt and pepper as needed. Enjoy right away or cover and chill in the fridge for a few hours until ready to serve.

# White Bean Chili

Serves 6

2 Tbsp olive oil

1 yellow onion, diced

1 green bell pepper, diced

1 jalapeño, finely diced

2 Tbsp all-purpose flour

3 garlic cloves, minced

2 tsp ground cumin

1 tsp ground coriander

1 tsp dried oregano

1 tsp smoked paprika

1 tsp salt

¼ tsp freshly ground black pepper

¼ tsp cayenne pepper

4 cups [960 ml] Homemade Roasted Vegetable Broth (page 209) or store-bought low-sodium vegetable broth

One 7 oz [200 g] can diced green chiles

Two 15 oz [430 g] cans white beans, such as cannellini or great Northern, rinsed

¾ cup [105 g] frozen corn

½ cup [120 ml] whole milk

4 oz [115 g] cream cheese

1 Tbsp fresh lime juice

## Topping Options

Pickled jalapeño slices

Tortilla chips or Fritos

Sliced avocado

Shredded Cheddar cheese

Hot sauce

## Meat Suggestion

Chicken is oftentimes found in white chili, so stirring in Shredded Chicken (page 217) would be very appropriate here. You could also top this with crumbled Candied Bacon (page 216).

Although red chilis tend to be more common, a white chili is perfect for when you are craving something rich, cheesy, and brimming with spices. This creamy recipe is a delicious vegetarian twist on traditional white chili with chicken, and it gets its creaminess from both milk and cream cheese swirled in at the end. Don't hold back on the topping options either. I love to add crunch with tortilla chips or Fritos, extra spice with hot sauce and pickled jalapeños, and richness with avocado and even more cheese.

1. In a large Dutch oven or stockpot over medium heat, warm the oil. Add the onion, bell pepper, and jalapeño and sauté until softened, about 7 minutes. Add the flour, garlic, cumin, coriander, oregano, paprika, salt, pepper, and cayenne and sauté until fragrant, 30 seconds.

2. Stir in 3 cups [720 ml] of the vegetable broth and the green chiles and bring to a boil over high heat.

3. Meanwhile, transfer 1 cup [160 g] of the white beans with ½ cup [120 ml] of the vegetable broth into a glass measuring cup or small bowl and use an immersion blender to purée (alternatively, transfer to a food processor or blender and blend). Once the soup is boiling, turn the heat down to medium-low. Add the puréed white beans, remaining whole white beans, and the corn and simmer for 15 minutes to develop the flavor.

4. Remove from the heat and stir in the milk, cream cheese, and lime juice. Taste and add salt as needed. If you like your chili a bit thinner, stir in the remaining ½ cup [120 ml] vegetable broth. Serve warm, with pickled jalapeños, tortilla chips, avocado, cheese, and hot sauce, if desired.

☞ **Pressure Cooker:** Using the sauté function on your pressure cooker, sauté the aromatics as in step 1. Turn the sauté setting off and add 2 cups [480 ml] of vegetable broth (instead of 3 cups [720 ml]) and the green chiles. Purée 1 cup [160 g] of the white beans with ½ cup [120 ml] of the vegetable broth and add to the soup along with the remaining whole beans and the corn. Pressure cook on high for 5 minutes, then quick release. Continue with the recipe from step 4.

☞ **Storing:** Store leftovers refrigerated in an airtight container for up to 3 days. I do not recommend freezing this chili due to the dairy.

# White Bean Hot Dish

**Serves 4 with a side
or 2 generously**

1 Tbsp olive oil

2 cups [215 g] finely chopped
cauliflower (from 1 small head)

2 garlic cloves, minced

¼ tsp salt

3 cups [720 ml] White Bean Chili
(page 155)

½ cup [40 g] shredded Monterey
Jack cheese

10 oz [285 g] frozen tater tots

A hot dish is a popular Northern Midwestern casserole usually containing a starch, meat, and some sort of canned soup. My version skips the meat and uses leftover White Bean Chili (page 155) as the base, but it doesn't skip the most popular starch topping: frozen tater tots. (Because let's be real—we all need to feed our tater tot cravings now and then!) I also fold in chopped cauliflower to help thicken the dish without altering the flavor too much.

1. Preheat the oven to 400°F [200°C]. In a large skillet over medium heat, warm the oil. Add the cauliflower, garlic, and salt and sauté until the cauliflower is starting to turn translucent, about 5 minutes. Remove from the heat and stir in the chili and cheese.

2. Transfer the mixture to a 9 in [23 cm] round baking dish and arrange the tater tots in a single layer on top, being careful not to push them too far into the filling.

3. Bake for 35 to 40 minutes, or until the tater tots are browned and the chili is bubbling around the edges of the dish. Cool slightly before serving. To store, let cool completely, cover with aluminum foil, and keep in the fridge for up to 2 days.

## Serves 9

### Strawberry-Rhubarb Champagne Soup

2 qt [960 g] strawberries

1½ cups (7 oz [200 g]) chopped rhubarb (from about 3 medium stalks)

½ cup [100 g] granulated sugar

1½ Tbsp cornstarch

1 Tbsp fresh lemon juice

1 cup [240 ml] chilled dry champagne

### Olive Oil Cake

1½ cups [210 g] all-purpose flour

½ Tbsp baking powder

¾ tsp salt

¼ tsp baking soda

¾ cup [150 g] granulated sugar

½ Tbsp grated lemon zest

2 eggs

1 cup [240 ml] buttermilk

¾ cup [180 ml] olive oil

1 Tbsp fresh lemon juice

### Strawberry Dust

1 oz [30 g] freeze-dried strawberries

### Mascarpone Whip

4 oz [115 g] mascarpone, very cold

½ cup [120 ml] heavy cream, very cold

½ cup [60 g] powdered sugar

1 Tbsp vanilla paste, or 1 tsp vanilla extract plus seeds from ½ vanilla bean

½ Tbsp honey

# Chilled Strawberry-Rhubarb Champagne Soup with Olive Oil Cake

After testing the nourishing winter and fall recipes for months on end, I was so excited to get to this spring soup. Most of the soups in the cooler weather chapters are meant to comfort you and your family during the dark and damp days, so it felt like such a wonderful mindshift to move onto a recipe that is made to be shared with friends on a sunny spring day.

This chilled dessert soup is meant to be served with a piece of the Olive Oil Cake in the center of a bowl and the soup poured around it. This essentially makes the soup a delicious sauce that should be enjoyed with each bite of cake. I like the extra pop that comes from sprinkling some strawberry dust (ground freeze-dried strawberries) over the mascarpone whip, but topping with additional fresh strawberries is also a great option.

My go-to drink of choice is champagne, and it was a no-brainer to use that here so I could serve what was left in the bottle to everyone as they enjoy their dessert. This recipe could also work with a chilled dry white wine if that is what you have on hand.

**1.** **Make the soup:** Slice 6 oz [170 g] of the strawberries and set aside. Quarter the rest and add them to a medium saucepan. Add the rhubarb, granulated sugar, and 1¾ cups [420 ml] of water (the liquid won't completely cover the fruit initially but will as the strawberries start to cook down). Bring to a boil over high heat, then turn the heat to medium-low and simmer for 5 minutes.

**2.** In a small bowl, mix the cornstarch with 3 Tbsp of cold water and then stir into the strawberry-rhubarb mixture. Simmer until thickened, about 5 minutes. Remove from the heat and add the reserved strawberries and the lemon juice. Use an immersion blender to blend until smooth. Transfer to an airtight container and chill in the fridge for at least 3 hours.

**continued** ☞

Quick Fix: Strawberry-Rhubarb Sauce p. 163

3. **Meanwhile, make the cake:** Preheat the oven to 350°F [180°C]. Grease an 8 in [20 cm] square baking pan and line the pan with parchment paper.

4. In a large bowl, whisk together the flour, baking powder, salt, and baking soda. In a medium bowl, whisk together the granulated sugar and lemon zest. Add the eggs and whisk until pale, about 1 minute. Add the buttermilk, oil, and lemon juice and whisk until combined. Make a well in the center of the dry ingredients and pour the wet ingredients into the center. Fold the dry ingredients into the wet until completely combined.

5. Pour the batter into the prepared baking pan and bake for 30 to 35 minutes, or until a toothpick inserted in the center comes out clean. Transfer to a cooling rack and cool completely before slicing into 9 even squares or circles (use a biscuit cutter if cutting into circles).

6. **Make the strawberry dust:** Place the freeze-dried strawberries in a high-speed blender and blend until completely broken up. Set aside.

7. **Make the mascarpone whip:** Add the mascarpone and cream to the bowl of a stand mixer fitted with a whisk attachment. Whisk on high until soft peaks form, 30 seconds to 1 minute. Turn the mixer to low and slowly add the powdered sugar and then the vanilla paste and honey. Turn the mixer up to medium and whisk until stiff peaks form, 1 minute or so. Transfer to a large zip-top bag and cut off one of the corners to use as a piping bag.

8. Place each piece of cake in the center of a soup bowl. Pipe some mascarpone whip over the top and then dust a little strawberry dust over the whip. Stir the champagne into the chilled soup. Pour some of the soup down the side of each bowl, making sure to avoid pouring it over the pieces of cake. Serve right away.

☞ **Storing:** Store leftover soup, cake, strawberry dust, and mascarpone whip refrigerated in separate airtight containers for up to 4 days or freeze for up to 3 months.

**Quick Fix**

Reduce leftover soup in a medium saucepan over medium heat until it is the consistency of maple syrup (time will vary depending on how much soup you have left). Drizzle over pancakes, waffles, crêpes, leftover cake, or ice cream.

# Gifting Soup

Instead of stashing leftovers away in your freezer, giving them away can be a nice option. Oftentimes, on Sundays, I'll make a double batch of soup that I portion out and split between weekly leftovers and gifting. It's thoughtful gift for anyone going through big life changes (a new job, a death in the family, etc.) or anyone with a busy schedule (a new baby, a hectic time at work). It's also just a really nice way to say "I'm thinking of you." To keep the effort minimal on the receiver's end, I usually just shoot them a text midday on Sunday along the lines of "I have some soup and an extra loaf of bread for you. OK for me to drop it off on your porch this evening?" This takes the pressure off the receiver to feel like they must invite you in, and also gives them the option to decline. I usually pack the soup in leftover take-out containers so there's no pressure to return the container to me. This casual gifting of soup requires no fussing over presentation (no bows, gift wrapping, or special plating) and is such a thoughtful and easy gesture. Many of the hearty salads and breads in the book (recipes start on page 219) also travel well and make great gifts alongside a soup.

# Gazpacho Verde with Ginger Vinaigrette

Serves 4 to 6

### Gazpacho Verde

2 lb [910 g] honeydew melon, peeled, seeds removed, and chopped into 1 in [2.5 cm] pieces (about 6 cups)

3 small seedless cucumbers, peeled and cut into 1 in [2.5 cm] pieces

1 avocado, peeled and seeded

1 bunch green onions, trimmed and coarsely chopped

1 bunch fresh cilantro, coarsely chopped

2 Tbsp pickled jalapeño slices plus 1 Tbsp pickling juice

Grated zest of 1 lime

1 Tbsp fresh lime juice

1 Tbsp white wine vinegar or champagne vinegar

½ tsp salt

¼ tsp freshly ground black pepper

2 Tbsp olive oil

### Ginger Vinaigrette

3 Tbsp olive oil

2 Tbsp white wine vinegar, champagne vinegar, or rice vinegar

1 tsp tamari

1 tsp grated fresh ginger

1 tsp brown sugar

1 tsp red pepper flakes

⅛ tsp salt

Sour cream or plain Greek yogurt, for serving (optional)

¼ cup [30 g] chopped roasted pistachios (optional)

This gazpacho is the dinner equivalent of a green smoothie for breakfast. Packed with fruits and veggies, it uses an abundance of in-season produce to create a meal that is light and delicious (something I can't always promise of my green smoothies). This no-cook soup comes together in minutes (plus chilling time) and hits all the right flavor notes for a summer meal: bright, acidic, herbaceous, and light.

1. **Make the gazpacho:** To the carafe of a blender, add the honeydew, cucumber, avocado, green onions, cilantro, pickled jalapeño and juice, lime zest and juice, vinegar, salt, and pepper and blend on high speed until very smooth, 3 to 5 minutes. Slowly pour in the oil while the blender is running, and blend for another 1 to 2 minutes, or until the soup is emulsified. Transfer to an airtight container and chill in the fridge for at least 2 hours.

2. **Meanwhile, make the ginger vinaigrette:** In a small bowl, whisk together oil, vinegar, tamari, ginger, brown sugar, red pepper flakes, and salt until emulsified. Taste and season with salt, pepper, and brown sugar as needed.

3. Taste the chilled soup and season as needed (it may need more salt, pepper, vinegar, or a dash of brown sugar to even out the flavor). Divide among serving bowls and top with a drizzle of the vinaigrette, a dollop of sour cream, and a sprinkle of pistachios, if desired. Serve right away.

☞ **Storing:** Store leftovers (without the sour cream or pistachios) refrigerated in an airtight container for up to 3 days or freeze for up to 3 months.

# Tomato-Cucumber Salad
# with Lemon Vinaigrette & Verde Sauce

**Serves 4 as a side**

### Goat Cheese Verde Sauce

4 oz [115 g] goat cheese

1 cup [240 g] plain whole Greek yogurt

½ cup [120 ml] Gazpacho Verde (page 169)

¼ tsp salt

⅛ tsp freshly ground black pepper

1 Tbsp olive oil

### Lemon Vinaigrette

1 Tbsp fresh lemon juice

1 tsp grated lemon zest

1 tsp honey

½ tsp red pepper flakes

¼ tsp salt

⅛ tsp freshly ground black pepper

¼ cup [60 ml] olive oil

### Salad

2 mini seedless cucumbers, halved and then each half cut into quarters

3 medium heirloom tomatoes (I like to choose a variety of colors), cored and cut into bite-size pieces

¼ cup [3 g] packed fresh mint, dill, or basil (or a mix of any)

¼ cup [30 g] chopped roasted pistachios

The key to this beautiful salad is layering, both for presentation and for building flavor. We start with a bed of smooth and tangy goat cheese verde sauce. We then toss crunchy and juicy vegetables in the bright and slightly spicy lemon vinaigrette and arrange them over the sauce. We top it all off with fresh soft herbs (use mint, dill, or basil or a mix depending on what is looking the freshest) and crunchy pistachios. To me, this is summer on a plate.

1.  **Make the verde sauce:** In a food processor fitted with the blade attachment, pulse the goat cheese a few times to break it up. Add the yogurt, gazpacho, salt, and pepper and pulse until completely combined, about 30 seconds. With the processor running, slowly stream in the oil. Spread the verde sauce evenly onto a serving plate and set aside.

2.  **Make the vinaigrette:** In a large bowl, whisk together the lemon juice and zest, honey, red pepper flakes, salt, and pepper. Whisking continuously, drizzle in the oil until emulsified. Pour half of the dressing into a small serving bowl and set aside.

3.  **Make the salad:** Transfer the cucumbers and tomatoes to the large bowl with the remaining vinaigrette and gently toss to coat.

4.  Arrange the vegetables over the verde sauce in a big heaping pile. Scatter the herbs and pistachios over the tomatoes and cucumbers. Serve right away, with the extra dressing on the side in case your guests like more heavily dressed salad.

# Tomato-Watermelon Gazpacho

Serves 6 to 8

12 oz [340 g] watermelon (from half a small melon), diced (about 2 cups)

2 lb [910 g] ripe red tomatoes (I usually use Roma), cored and diced

2 celery stalks, roughly chopped

1 red bell pepper, roughly chopped

3 green onions, roughly chopped

¼ cup [30 g] pickled jalapeño slices plus 1 Tbsp juice

½ tsp salt

2 Tbsp olive oil

### Meat Suggestion

I don't advise turning your oven on, but if you must, some crumbled Candied Bacon (page 216) would be a lovely topping on this gazpacho.

### Quick Fix

Add cold cooked noodles to bulk up this gazpacho (I like spaghetti or soba for this), along with bite-size pieces of veggies like cucumbers, bell peppers, green onions, and olives.

Wait to make this gazpacho until it's the scorching second half of summer when your farmers' market is bursting with juicy tomatoes, and it's just way too dang hot to go near your stove. I love using pickled jalapeños in this, as it adds both acid and spice (I really like the brand Rio Luna; they're also delicious on nachos, tacos, and salads if you have any left over). I don't like things too spicy, so this has a mild kick, but feel free to use more pickled jalapeños or even add some hot sauce at the end if you prefer. For more texture, toss in some additional diced tomatoes and watermelon when serving.

1. Add the watermelon to a blender, blend on high until smooth, and strain through a fine-mesh strainer into a bowl. Discard the solids and pour the watermelon juice back into the blender. Add the tomatoes, celery, bell pepper, green onions, pickled jalapeño and juice, and salt. Blend on high speed until completely smooth, 3 to 5 minutes. With the blender running, slowly pour in the oil and blend for an additional 2 to 3 minutes, or until emulsified. Taste and season with salt and jalapeño juice as needed. Transfer to an airtight container and chill at least 2 hours before serving.

☞ Storing: Store leftovers refrigerated in an airtight container for up to 4 days or freeze for up to 2 months.

# Bloody Maria with Quick-Pickled Watermelon Wedges

Serves 2

### Quick-Pickled Watermelon Wedges

10 oz [280 g] watermelon, cut into thick wedges

1 cup [240 ml] rice vinegar

¼ cup [50 g] sugar

1 tsp red pepper flakes

¼ tsp salt

### Bloody Marias

2 cups [480 ml] Tomato-Watermelon Gazpacho (page 173)

2 Tbsp pickle juice

1 Tbsp fresh lemon juice

2 tsp vegetarian Worcestershire sauce

1 tsp hot sauce

1 tsp prepared horseradish

½ tsp celery salt

¼ tsp freshly ground black pepper

2 to 3 oz [60 to 90 ml] tequila

The Tomato-Watermelon Gazpacho (page 173) is so flavorful that it really doesn't need much dressing up to turn it into the perfect cocktail mixer. I do add a little umami and celery salt to make it taste a bit more like a traditional Bloody Mary, but I don't do much beyond that. I've found that people have really strong opinions about their Bloody Mary preferences, so I'd recommend you taste and adjust as you add each ingredient to come to a balance that resonates with you.

Since you already have pickled jalapeños on hand from making the gazpacho, feel free to use them as the pickle juice in this recipe. These are made with tequila to make them Bloody Marias, but I won't be offended if you prefer to swap in vodka. The recipe is easy to double or triple depending on how much gazpacho you have left over.

1. **Make the quick-pickled watermelon wedges:** Place the watermelon wedges in a wide bowl in a single layer. To a small saucepan, add the vinegar, 1 cup [240 ml] of water, the sugar, red pepper flakes, and salt. Bring to a boil over high heat, stirring often to help the sugar dissolve. Remove the brine from the heat and pour over the watermelon, making sure the wedges are completely submerged. Transfer to the fridge and chill for at least 20 minutes and up to an hour. Don't leave overnight, as the acidic brine may break down the watermelon too much over time.

2. **Make the Bloody Marias:** In a large pitcher, stir together the gazpacho, pickle juice, lemon juice, Worcestershire, hot sauce, horseradish, celery salt, and pepper. Taste and adjust the seasoning to your liking. Stir in the tequila.

3. Fill two highball glasses with ice and then divide the mixture between them. Serve right away, with pickled watermelon wedges.

# Summer Garden Minestrone

Serves 8

2 Tbsp olive oil

1 white onion, diced

2 carrots, peeled and diced

2 celery stalks, diced

4 garlic cloves, minced

1 tsp fresh thyme leaves

2 Tbsp dried oregano

1 tsp salt

1 tsp red pepper flakes

1 lb [455 g] Roma tomatoes,
cored and chopped

¼ cup [55 g] tomato paste

8 cups [2 L] Homemade Roasted
Vegetable Broth (page 209)
or store-bought low-sodium
vegetable broth

12 oz [340 g] zucchini or yellow
squash, diced

1 bay leaf

1 cup [85 g] small pasta shapes,
such as orecchiette or orzo

One 15¾ oz [450 g] can great
Northern beans, rinsed

One 15¾ oz [450 g] can red
kidney beans, rinsed

6 oz [170 g] green beans,
cut into 2 in [5 cm] pieces

1 Tbsp fresh lemon juice

Freshly ground black pepper,
to taste

Green Romesco (page 213) and
grated Parmesan cheese, for
serving

### Meat Suggestion

Although we usually think of burgers
when we think of summertime
beef, Mini Meatballs (page 217) are
a wonderful way to bulk up this
warm-weather soup.

The ingredient list for this soup may look intimidating, but I'm betting you already have most of these items on hand. You should be able to grab the rest at any farmers' market in the summer months. Although it's traditional to serve minestrone with a pesto (since both are Italian), I love the heat and smokiness that comes from the charred peppers in the Green Romesco (page 213).

1. In a large Dutch oven or stockpot over medium heat, warm the oil. Add the onion, carrots, and celery and sauté until softened, 5 to 7 minutes. Add the garlic, thyme, oregano, salt, and red pepper flakes and sauté until fragrant, 30 seconds. Add the tomatoes and tomato paste and sauté until most of the liquid from the tomatoes has evaporated, about 5 minutes. Add the vegetable broth, zucchini, and bay leaf and bring to a boil over high heat. Cover, lower the heat to medium-low, and simmer for at least 45 minutes to develop flavor.

2. Bring a large pot of salted water to a boil and cook the pasta according to the package directions. Drain and set aside.

3. Uncover the minestrone and add the great Northern beans, kidney beans, and green beans. Cover and simmer until the green beans are tender, about 5 minutes. Remove from the heat and let sit for 5 minutes, still covered. Add the lemon juice and then taste and season with salt and pepper as needed.

4. Divide the soup among individual bowls and ladle in a scoop of pasta. Swirl in a spoonful of Green Romesco and sprinkle with Parmesan.

☞ Storing: Store leftovers refrigerated in an airtight container for up to 3 days or freeze for up to 2 months.

**Quick Fix**

Make ricotta toast for an easy lunch! Warm 1 cup [240 ml] leftover minestrone to 165°F [75°C] and then strain through a fine-mesh strainer, discarding the liquid. Whip ¾ cup [180 g] whole-milk ricotta with a pinch of salt in a blender or food processor until light and fluffy (alternatively, whip with a whisk in a small bowl for easier cleanup but less fluffy ricotta). Spread the ricotta evenly on top of two pieces of toasted bread and then top each piece with 1 Tbsp leftover Green Romesco (page 213), followed by the strained veggies. Serve right away.

Quick Fix: Ricotta Toast p. 181

# Loaded Quinoa Burgers

Serves 6

½ cup [90 g] quinoa, rinsed

1½ cups [360 ml] Summer Garden Minestrone (page 181) (pasta reserved for another use)

½ cup [30 g] panko bread crumbs

¼ cup [35 g] finely diced onion

¼ cup [8 g] grated Parmesan cheese

3 Tbsp ricotta

2 Tbsp chopped fresh parsley

1 Tbsp tomato paste

1 tsp garlic powder

½ tsp salt

¼ tsp freshly ground black pepper

1 egg, lightly beaten

1 Tbsp olive oil

6 slices Cheddar cheese (optional)

6 burger buns

Topping Options

Mayonnaise

Ketchup

Mustard

Barbecue sauce

Shredded lettuce

Pickle slices

It's summer, which means it's burger season! These quinoa burgers are made in the oven but can be baked ahead and reheated on the grill if you are having a cookout. Just be gentle when putting them on the grill, as they are fragile compared to store-bought veggie burgers. I also recommend brushing them with a little oil on both sides so they don't stick to the grill. If I'm having guests over, I like to serve these with potato salad and corn on the cob. For a more casual approach, I've also been known to bake up a bag of frozen tater tots as the side dish.

1. In a small saucepan, combine the quinoa with 1 cup [240 ml] of water and bring to a boil over high heat. Cover, lower the heat to medium-low, and simmer until all the water has absorbed and the quinoa is tender, about 15 minutes. Remove from the heat and let sit, covered, for 5 minutes.

2. Preheat the oven to 400°F [200°C] and line a baking sheet with parchment paper.

3. Drain the minestrone and discard the liquid. Finely dice any large chunks of vegetables or beans so they incorporate into the patties more easily. Add the minestrone solids to a large bowl and use a potato masher or a fork to gently mash. Add the bread crumbs, onion, Parmesan, ricotta, parsley, tomato paste, garlic powder, salt, and pepper. Add the cooked quinoa and mix to combine. Add the egg and mix until incorporated.

4. Using clean hands and a measuring cup, scoop out ½ cup [115 g] of the mixture, gently press into a round patty, and transfer to the prepared baking sheet. Repeat with the rest of the mixture until you have six evenly spaced patties on your baking sheet. Brush the patties with the oil and bake for 25 minutes, or until browned on top and cooked all the way through. If grilling, bake for 20 minutes and finish out on the grill.

5. If making cheeseburgers, add a slice of cheese over each burger during the last 2 minutes of baking (or add the cheese while the burgers reheat on the grill). Serve the patties on the burger buns with all your favorite toppings and sauces.

# Baba Ghanoush-Inspired Eggplant Soup

**Serves 4**

2 lb [910 g] eggplants (about 2 medium)

½ cup [90 g] pearled farro, rinsed

2 cups [480 ml] Homemade Roasted Vegetable Broth (page 209) or store-bought low-sodium vegetable broth

⅓ cup [75 g] tahini

3 Tbsp fresh lemon juice

2 Tbsp plain Greek yogurt

½ Tbsp ground cumin

1 tsp smoked paprika

2 garlic cloves, grated

¼ cup [60 ml] olive oil

Salt, to taste

Freshly ground black pepper, to taste

**Cumin Oil**

2 Tbsp olive oil

2 tsp cumin seeds

**Quick Fix**

Swirl in some Green Tahini (page 212) after reheating the soup.

Since eggplants abound during warmer months, I knew I wanted to include an eggplant soup in the summer section of this book. My favorite way to enjoy eggplant is when it's blended with lots of spices and creamy tahini into an irresistible baba ghanoush. Thus, my inspiration for this soup was born. It's essentially a thinned-out, velvety soup form of smoky baba ganoush with chewy farro and a cumin oil drizzle. Use high-quality tahini and fresh eggplant to avoid too much bitterness creeping in. I love serving this with Quick Yogurt Flatbread (page 235) or store-bought naan.

1. Preheat a gas or charcoal grill to medium heat. Or, if you don't have a grill, you can use the broiler function in your oven; preheat on high. Poke holes all over the eggplants and place directly on the grill grates, or on a baking sheet if broiling. Cook, turning often with tongs, until the eggplants are charred all over and soft all the way through, about 30 minutes. Remove from the heat and set aside until cool enough to handle.

2. Meanwhile, bring 4 cups [960 ml] of salted water to a boil in a large pot over high heat. Add the farro, lower the heat to medium-low, and simmer until tender, 20 to 25 minutes. Drain and set aside.

3. Cut open the eggplants and scoop out the flesh, discarding the skins. Transfer the eggplant flesh to a blender along with the vegetable broth, tahini, lemon juice, yogurt, cumin, paprika, and garlic. Blend on high speed until smooth, about 2 minutes. With the blender running, slowly stream in the oil and blend until the oil is completely incorporated.

4. Transfer the eggplant mixture to a medium saucepan and gently bring to a simmer over medium-low heat. Stir in the farro and remove from the heat. Taste and season with salt, pepper, and lemon juice as needed.

5. Make the cumin oil: Combine the oil and cumin seeds in a small skillet over medium heat. Cook until the cumin seeds are fragrant and starting to darken, about 1 minute. Remove from the heat and spoon over the soup to serve.

☞ Storing: Store leftover soup and cumin oil separately refrigerated in airtight containers for up to 3 days or freeze the soup for up to 2 months.

# Corn & Roasted Poblano Chowder

Serves 4 to 6

4 ears corn, husks and silks removed

4 cups [960 ml] Homemade Roasted Vegetable Broth (page 209) or store-bought low-sodium vegetable broth

1 bay leaf

1 tsp whole coriander seeds

1 tsp whole cumin seeds

1 tsp black peppercorns

¾ tsp salt

4 poblano peppers

4 Tbsp [55 g] unsalted butter

1 white onion, diced

2 celery stalks, diced

1 serrano chile, diced very small and seeds removed (optional, add only if you like a lot of heat)

2 garlic cloves, minced

3 Tbsp all-purpose flour

1 russet potato, peeled and cut into ¾ in [2 cm] dice

1 cup [240 ml] half-and-half

1 Tbsp fresh lime juice

Pinch of sugar (optional)

Chopped fresh chives, for serving

Meat Suggestion

Some salty-sweet crumbled Candied Bacon (page 216) would be a delicious topping in addition to the chopped chives.

I could have made an entire chapter just out of corn recipes. My love of corn stems from growing up in the Midwest with a corn-field in my backyard. I begin to crave it as soon as the harvest starts showing up at the market.

For this book, I played around with a few different corn and poblano recipes (one of my favorite combos), but I always came back to this rather traditional chowder. Infusing the broth with the corn cobs and additional whole spices brings extra depth to the soup without too much extra work.

Only add the serrano if you like a lot of heat. I recommend using disposable gloves when chopping the poblanos and serrano to avoid the irritating tingling that may occur on your hands caused by capsaicin (speaking from experience here!).

1. Hold 1 ear of corn upright in a wide, shallow bowl and use a sharp knife to cut the kernels off the cob. Repeat with the remaining ears.

2. Snap the cobs in half and put them in a medium saucepan. Add the vegetable broth, 1 cup [240 ml] of water, the bay leaf, coriander seeds, cumin seeds, peppercorns, and ¼ tsp of the salt. Bring to a boil over high heat, then lower the heat to medium-low, cover, and simmer the broth for 30 minutes.

3. Meanwhile, cook the poblanos on an outdoor grill (heated to medium) or in the broiler, turning often, until they are evenly charred on all sides, 8 to 10 minutes. Transfer to a large zip-top bag, seal, and let the peppers cool completely in the bag. When the poblanos are cool enough to handle, remove the charred skin, rinse them, remove the seeds, and cut into ¾ in [2 cm] pieces.

continued ☞

4. When the broth has 10 minutes of cooking time left, in a large Dutch oven or saucepan over medium heat, melt the butter. Add the onions and celery and sauté for 5 minutes. Add the corn kernels, serrano (if using), and poblano pieces and sauté until the poblano pieces are starting to soften, 3 minutes. Add the garlic and sauté until fragrant, 30 seconds. Add the flour, stirring to make sure the flour coats all the vegetables, and sauté for 1 minute.

5. Strain the broth through a fine-mesh strainer set over a heat-proof bowl, discarding the solids. Transfer the broth to the Dutch oven along with the potatoes and the remaining ½ tsp of salt. Bring to a boil, then lower the heat to medium-low and simmer for 10 minutes, stirring often to keep the potatoes from falling to the bottom of the pan and sticking.

6. Remove from the heat and stir in the half-and-half and lime juice. Once cool enough to taste, season with salt and lime juice as needed. Add a pinch of sugar if your corn wasn't very sweet. Serve, topped with a sprinkle of chives.

☞ **Storing:** Store leftovers refrigerated in an airtight container for up to 3 days. I do not recommend freezing this soup, as the texture gets compromised in the process.

# Corn & Roasted Poblano Fritters

**Serves 2**

1 cup [240 ml] Corn &
Roasted Poblano Chowder
(page 189), drained

1 cup [140 g] fresh or
frozen corn kernels

2 oz [55 g] Cheddar cheese,
shredded

2 eggs, lightly beaten

1 Tbsp chopped fresh chives

½ tsp salt

¼ tsp freshly ground
black pepper

⅔ cup [90 g] all-purpose flour

Cooking oil, such as
olive or peanut, for frying

Salsa or Hot Honey Sour Cream
(see page 192), for serving

I'm a big fan of making these fritters for lunch but these could easily be bulked up into a light summer dinner option with the addition of a side salad.

1. In a large mixing bowl, whisk together drained chowder, corn, Cheddar, eggs, chives, salt, and pepper. Fold in the flour. Add enough oil to cover the bottom of a small skillet and warm it over medium heat.

2. Drop ¼ cup [60 ml] of the batter into the pan, use a spoon to gently press down on the batter to spread it out, and cook until golden on both sides and cooked all the way through, 2 to 3 minutes on each side.

3. Line a plate with paper towels. Transfer the cooked fritters to the prepared plate to drain. Repeat with the rest of the batter. You should end up with about ten fritters. These are best enjoyed warm with salsa or Hot Honey Sour Cream.

# Savory Corn-Poblano Pudding

Serves 4 as a main
or 6 to 8 as a side

⅓ cup [80 ml] half-and-half

2 Tbsp unsalted butter, melted
and cooled

1 Tbsp cornstarch

2 oz [55 g] Cheddar or pepper
Jack cheese, shredded

3 eggs

1 Tbsp chopped fresh chives

½ tsp salt

¼ tsp freshly ground black
pepper

1 cup [140 g] fresh or frozen corn

1½ cups [360 ml] Corn &
Roasted Poblano Chowder
(page 189)

**Hot Honey Sour Cream**

½ cup [120 g] sour cream

1 Tbsp honey (I prefer the mild
flavor of clover honey here)

½ Tbsp hot sauce, plus more for
serving

Pinch of salt

Corn casserole is always my favorite Thanksgiving side, and I've often wondered why we reserve it for the holiday season. I'm hoping to change that mindset, so I've started to make this corn pudding in the summer, when corn is actually at its peak. This version is a bit more egg-heavy than the usual holiday side; I find it works perfectly as an easy vegetarian main dish since it borders on frittata territory. Serve this at brunch with a simple side salad (I've got lots of options for you in the Accompaniments section, starting on page 219) or as a side at your next cookout.

It's not mandatory, but the simple Hot Honey Sour Cream is delicious dolloped onto a serving of both this and the fritters on page 191. Hot sauces vary widely in spice levels, so use whichever one is your favorite and start with less, taste, and add more as needed.

1. Preheat the oven to 350°F [180°C] and grease an 8 in [20 cm] square baking pan. In a medium bowl, whisk together the half-and-half, butter, cornstarch, half of the cheese, the eggs, chives, salt, and pepper. Add the corn and soup and fold until incorporated.

2. Transfer the mixture to the prepared baking pan and sprinkle the remaining cheese over the top. Bake for 30 to 35 minutes, or until set. Turn on the broiler and broil for 1 minute, or until the top has browned (watching closely to make sure the top doesn't get too hard). Remove from the oven and cool on a wire rack for a few minutes.

3. Meanwhile, make the hot honey sour cream: Whisk together the sour cream, honey, hot sauce, and salt. Taste and add more hot sauce or honey if needed.

4. Cut the corn pudding into squares and serve warm with the honey sour cream on the side.

Serves 4

**Marshmallow Meringue**

3 egg whites

¾ cup [150 g] granulated sugar

½ tsp vanilla extract

¼ tsp cream of tartar

**Graham Cracker Dust**

½ cup [60 g] crushed graham crackers

**Dark Chocolate Soup**

1 Tbsp cornstarch

2 cups [480 ml] whole milk

1 cup [240 ml] heavy cream

2 Tbsp powdered sugar

½ tsp salt

1 egg yolk

8 oz [230 g] bitter chocolate, at least 70%, chopped

# Dark Chocolate S'mores Soup

This luscious chocolate soup sits somewhere between a pudding and syrup and is fantastic served to guests as a light summer dessert. Dark chocolate keeps the soup from becoming too sweet, while the whip keeps the whole dessert light. The dust adds texture. Although it's not necessary, if you have a kitchen torch, you could torch the meringue a bit before serving to add some color.

"Graham cracker dust" is just a fancy way of saying you crumbled a few graham crackers over the meringue to make it taste like deconstructed s'mores. Your guests don't need to know it's that simple, right?

**1.** Make the marshmallow meringue: In a medium bowl set over a saucepan of simmering water, whisk the egg whites with the granulated sugar until the whites are warm and the sugar has dissolved, 2 to 3 minutes. Transfer the egg whites to the bowl of a stand mixer fitted with the whisk attachment and add the vanilla and cream of tartar. Beat on medium speed until firm, about 1 minute, and then increase to high and beat until stiff and glossy, 5 to 7 minutes. Transfer to the fridge to keep cold until ready to serve.

**2.** Make the graham cracker dust: Add the crushed graham crackers to a blender and blend into a fine dust, about 20 seconds.

**3.** Make the dark chocolate soup: In a small bowl, whisk together the cornstarch and 1 Tbsp of cold water and set aside. In a medium saucepan over medium heat, warm the milk, cream, powdered sugar, and salt, whisking often. Heat the mixture until bubbles start to form along the edges of the pan, but not to the point that it starts to simmer; lower the heat if needed to keep from simmering. Whisk in the cornstarch mixture. In the empty bowl used for the cornstarch, whisk the egg yolk. Remove ½ cup [120 ml] of the warmed milk mixture from the saucepan and slowly pour it into the bowl with the egg, whisking continuously to keep the egg from scrambling. Whisk the egg-milk mixture back into the saucepan. Cook until the liquid has thickened and easily coats the back of a spoon, 5 to 7 minutes.

**continued** ☞

**4.** Remove from the heat and add the chopped chocolate. Let sit
for a minute to allow the chocolate to melt and then whisk to
completely incorporate the chocolate into the milk mixture.

**5.** Divide the soup among dessert bowls and top each with
a heaping mound of marshmallow meringue. Torch the
meringue with a kitchen torch until dark on top. Add 2 tsp of
graham cracker dust over each meringue. Enjoy right away.

☞ Storing: Store leftovers refrigerated in individual airtight
containers for up to 2 days. I do not recommend freezing this
due to the dairy.

Quick Fix: Chocolate Dip (facing page)

# Triple-Chocolate Rye Brownies

**Makes 24 brownies**

11 Tbsp [155 g] unsalted butter

1¼ cup [300 ml] Dark Chocolate
S'mores Soup (page 197)

1 cup [110 g] rye flour

½ cup [70 g] all-purpose flour

½ cup [40 g] Dutch-process
cocoa powder

1 tsp salt

½ tsp baking powder

4 eggs

1 cup [200 g] packed brown
sugar

2 tsp vanilla extract

¾ cup [135 g] chocolate chips

These deeply chocolatey brownies get their flavor from three angles: the chocolate soup, the cocoa powder, and the chocolate chips. The rye flour brings a lovely earthiness to counterbalance the sweet without overpowering the flavor.

1. Preheat the oven to 350°F [180°C] and grease a 9 by 13 in [23 by 33 cm] baking pan.

2. Combine the butter and soup in a medium saucepan. Warm over medium-low heat, whisking often, until the butter is melted and incorporated into the chocolate. Remove from the heat and set aside to cool for at least 10 minutes.

3. In a medium bowl, whisk together the rye flour, all-purpose flour, cocoa powder, salt, and baking powder. Set aside.

4. In the bowl of a stand mixer fitted with the paddle attachment, whisk the eggs, brown sugar, and vanilla together on medium-high speed until shiny and smooth, about 3 minutes. Stream the cooled chocolate-butter mixture into the eggs and whisk until incorporated, 30 seconds. Use a spatula to fold the dry ingredients into the wet just until no dry bits remain. Fold in the chocolate chips.

5. Pour the batter into the prepared baking pan and use a spatula to spread it into an even layer. Bake for 17 to 20 minutes, or until the center is just barely wobbly. Cool completely on a wire rack before slicing and serving. Store leftovers in an airtight container at room temperature for up to 3 days.

# Setting a Soup Tablescape

Although it's easy to host a casual soup hang (see page 121 for hosting a soup swap), there are times when you just want to go all out and pamper your friends and family with a sit-down meal that can be lingered over at length with lively conversation and a few bottles of wine. If you're hoping to set a beautiful table and host an elegant soup party, here are some tips.

Use a linen or light-colored tablecloth and/or a table runner. Cluster some candles and a flower arrangement in the middle of the table. When setting a tablescape where the soup will be the main entrée, skip the large dinner plates and instead set out salad plates and big shallow bowls. Place a soup spoon and a knife to the right of the soup bowl and a fork and linen napkin to the left. Above the place setting, set wine and water glasses slightly to the right. A bread plate and butter knife go on the left of the setting. Once you've completed your main courses, remove all the dishes and bring out new dessert bowls and spoons along with coffee cups if serving coffee or tea with dessert.

For simplicity and ease, present the food family-style, with sliced bread on a bread board, salads in big serving bowls with tongs, and the soup in a Dutch oven with a potholder under it and a ladle. If you are worried about the Dutch oven being too heavy to pass around the table, plate just the soup in the kitchen and make a big show of bringing it out and presenting each bowl in front of your guests. Then let them serve themselves with all the side items (bread, salad, and so on).

Red Cabbage Soup with Crème Fraîche & Dill p. 131

# A Few Menu Ideas

## FALL

**Starter**
A cheeseboard with Honeyed Feta with Black & White Sesame Seeds (page 214), a blue cheese wedge, toasted pecans, grapes, and chocolate pieces

**Salad**
229    Brussels Sprouts Salad with Apple Cider Vinaigrette

**Bread**
239    Green Olive & Rosemary Focaccia

**Soup**
47    White Bean Stew with Marinated Radicchio

**Dessert**
197    Dark Chocolate S'mores Soup

## WINTER

**Starter**
227    Citrus Salad with Rosemary Candied Walnuts & Radicchio

**Salad**
231    Winter Farro Salad with Agrodolce Sauce

**Bread**
241    Cheddar & Pickled Jalapeño Dutch Oven Bread

**Soup**
101    Roasted Root Vegetable & Dumpling Soup

**Dessert**
197    Dark Chocolate S'mores Soup as a dip—skip the meringue and instead serve with orange segments for dipping

## SPRING

**Starter**
214    Crostini with Citrus-Artichoke White Pesto and blanched spring peas and asparagus pieces

**Salad**
223    Kale Salad with Parsley-Lemon Vinaigrette

**Bread**
237    Sun-Dried Tomato & Manchego Biscuits

**Soup**
151    Spring Vegetable Chowder

**Dessert**
161    Chilled Strawberry-Rhubarb Champagne Soup with Olive Oil Cake

## SUMMER

**Starter**
213    Green Romesco served as a dip with cherry tomatoes, bell pepper pieces, and carrots

**Salad**
221    Italian-ish Chopped Salad with Apricot-Oregano Dressing

**Bread**
233    Lemon-Poppyseed Popovers

**Soup**
181    Summer Garden Minestrone

**Dessert**
173    Tomato-Watermelon Gazpacho, served with a drizzle of honey to sweeten it up a bit

# SOUP ENHANCERS

**Makes about 9 cups [2.1 L]**

4 carrots, peeled and cut
into 1½ in [4 cm] pieces

2 yellow onions, peeled and
quartered

5 celery stalks, cut into 1½ in
[4 cm] pieces

1 garlic head, halved crosswise
so the cloves are visible

1 lb [455 g] white button
mushrooms, halved

1 tsp olive oil

½ tsp salt

1 bunch fresh parsley

5 thyme sprigs

1 Tbsp black peppercorns

1 Tbsp tomato paste

2 bay leaves

# Homemade Roasted Vegetable Broth

I always have homemade vegetable broth stashed in my freezer. I freeze the broth in an ice cube tray and then store the cubes in freezer-safe containers in the freezer. Make sure to note how much broth your tray holds, so you know how many cubes to use when cooking. (With my tray, eight ice cubes equals 1 cup [240 ml] of broth.)

I purposefully keep my vegetable broth very light on salt. This allows me to control how much salt I'm using so I don't end up with an oversalted soup.

**1.** Preheat the oven to 400°F [200°C]. Place the carrots, onions, celery, garlic, and mushrooms on a baking sheet and toss to coat with the oil and ¼ tsp of the salt. Roast for 45 minutes, or until soft and browned.

**2.** Transfer the roasted vegetables into a large Dutch oven or stockpot (make sure to scrape up and add any browned bits that are stuck to the pan). Add 4 qt [3.8 L] of water, the parsley, thyme, peppercorns, tomato paste, bay leaves, and the remaining ¼ tsp of the salt. Bring to a boil over high heat and then lower the heat to medium-low and simmer for 1 hour to develop the flavor.

**3.** Strain the broth through a fine-mesh strainer into a heat-proof bowl. Discard the cooked vegetables and herbs. Use right away or let the broth cool slightly before transferring to airtight containers in the fridge or freezer.

☞ **Pressure Cooker:** Roast the vegetables as in step 1. When you get to step 2, transfer the vegetables and remaining ingredients to a pressure cooker and add 12 cups [2.8 L] water (or fill to the maximum fill line, if less). Pressure cook on high for 25 minutes, then quick release. Continue from step 3.

☞ **Slow Cooker:** Roast the vegetables as described in step 1. When you get to step 2, transfer the roasted vegetables and remaining ingredients to a slow cooker and add 12 cups [2.8 L] of water (or fill to the maximum fill line, if less). Cover and slow cook on high for 4 hours. Continue from step 3.

☞ **Storing:** Store refrigerated in airtight containers for up to 5 days or freeze for up to 3 months.

# Cheater Vegetable Broth

### Makes about 4 cups [960 ml]

I fully realize that the vegetable broth recipe I gave you on the previous page takes 2 hours to execute. We don't always have that much time to spend in the kitchen, so I use this shortcut "cheater" vegetable broth when I need a smaller amount quickly. This recipe utilizes store-bought vegetable broth jazzed up with vegetables, herbs, and spices. Don't skip adding a tomato or tomato paste; it adds a burst of umami. Because some of the broth will evaporate as it cooks, I like to add back a little water so that it doesn't get too salty and because many of my recipes call for 4 cups [960 ml] of broth.

4 cups [960 ml] store-bought low-sodium vegetable broth

1 yellow onion, peeled and quartered

2 celery stalks, cut into 2 in [5 cm] pieces

1 carrot, peeled and cut into 2 in [5 cm] pieces

1 plum tomato, chopped, or ½ Tbsp tomato paste

4 thyme or parsley sprigs

2 garlic cloves, peeled and lightly smashed

1 tsp whole peppercorns

1 bay leaf

½ Tbsp champagne vinegar or rice vinegar

**I.** Add the vegetable broth, onion, celery, carrot, tomato, herbs, garlic, peppercorns, bay leaf, and ½ cup [120 ml] of water to a large stockpot and bring to a boil over high heat. Lower the heat to medium-low and simmer for at least 30 minutes to develop flavor. Remove from the heat and use a fine-mesh strainer over a large bowl to strain out the solids to discard. Stir in the vinegar.

☞ **Storing:** Let the broth cool slightly, then store refrigerated in an airtight container for up to 5 days or freeze for up to 3 months.

# Tarragon-Orange Oil

### Makes ½ cup [120 ml]

This bright, herbaceous oil adds both color and vibrancy to soups. Add a few drops to make an impact on the flavor of your soup. Double or triple this recipe if you want to keep it around to top salads or fried eggs.

½ cup [6 g] packed tarragon leaves

Grated zest of 2 navel oranges (about 1 Tbsp packed)

½ cup [120 ml] olive oil

⅛ tsp salt

**I.** Make an ice bath by adding 1 cup [220 g] of ice to a small bowl and filling it three-quarters full with cold water. Bring a medium saucepan of water to a boil over high heat. Add the tarragon and blanch for 45 seconds. Use a slotted spoon to transfer the tarragon to the ice bath. Cool in the ice bath for 1 minute. Use the slotted spoon to transfer the tarragon to a paper towel and pat dry. Transfer to a high-speed blender along with the orange zest, oil, and salt. Blend on high speed until the tarragon is completely chopped up and the oil is bright green, 3 to 5 minutes.

**2.** Strain through a fine-mesh strainer or cheesecloth and discard the solids. Use the oil right away or transfer to an airtight container. Let come to room temperature before storing.

☞ **Storing:** Store in an airtight container in the fridge for up to 1 week.

# Cider-Mustard Glaze

**Makes about ½ cup [120 ml]**

I love having a batch of this glaze on hand during the fall months to drizzle over soups, roasted veggies, and salads.

1 cup [240 ml] apple cider
2 Tbsp unsalted butter
1 tsp ground mustard
Pinch of salt

1. In a small skillet over medium heat, simmer the apple cider until reduced by half, 10 to 12 minutes. Remove from the heat and whisk in the butter, mustard, and salt. Whisk until emulsified.

☞ **Storing:** Let cool before storing in an airtight container in the fridge for up to 1 week.

# Frizzled Shallots

**Makes about 1 cup [35 g]**

Sometimes soup needs a little crunch. These frizzled shallots always do the job. Top your soup right before eating to keep them crisp. Watch them closely while cooking because the time they take to turn golden will vary greatly depending on the size of your shallot rings and how quickly your pan heats up. As soon as they've taken on a golden-brown color, remove from the heat immediately.

½ cup [120 ml] vegetable, canola, or olive oil
4 small or 2 large shallots,
peeled and sliced into ⅛ in [3 mm] rings
¼ tsp salt

1. Line a plate with paper towels. Warm the oil in a small skillet over medium heat. Add the shallots and simmer in the oil, stirring often, until golden brown, 10 to 15 minutes. Remove from the heat and strain through a fine-mesh strainer placed over a medium bowl. Discard the oil or save for another use. Transfer the shallots to the paper towel–lined plate and sprinkle with salt. The shallots will crisp up as they cool.

☞ **Storing:** Frizzled Shallots are best enjoyed the same day but can be stored in an airtight container at room temperature for up to 3 days.

# Green Tahini

**Makes about 1 cup [220 g]**

If you are a fan of tahini, you are going to love this simple sauce. Swirl it into puréed soups for an extra boost of flavor or use as a dressing on salads. Top with sesame seeds for extra crunch.

½ cup [110 g] tahini

½ cup [6 g] packed fresh cilantro

¼ cup [3 g] packed fresh parsley

2 Tbsp fresh lime juice

1 garlic clove, peeled

½ tsp ground cumin

⅛ tsp salt

1 tsp sesame seeds (optional)

**1.** Transfer the tahini, cilantro, parsley, lime juice, garlic, cumin, salt, and ½ cup [120 ml] water to a blender and blend until smooth and bright green. Drizzle into your favorite soups and sprinkle with toasted sesame seeds, if desired.

☞ **Storing:** Store (without the sesame seeds) in an airtight container in the fridge for up to 4 days.

# Green Apple-Mint Chutney

**Makes 1 cup [300 g]**

I love the triple hit of sweet, spicy, and bright in this chutney. I kept this at a medium heat for my personal taste, but feel free to add more chile or leave in the seeds if you like more spice.

1 Granny Smith apple, peeled, cored, and cut into 2 in [5 cm] chunks

1 Tbsp grated fresh ginger

2 Tbsp fresh lime juice

1 fresh green chile, diced (remove the seeds if you don't like too much heat)

½ tsp salt

1 bunch fresh mint (about 1 cup packed [12 g])

1 large bunch fresh cilantro (about 3 cups packed [36 g])

**1.** To the carafe of a high-speed blender, add the apple chunks, ginger, lime juice, green chile, and salt and blend until smooth. Add the mint and cilantro and blend for just a few seconds so that the leaves are mixed in and chopped but not completely incorporated. Taste and season with salt and lime juice as needed.

☞ **Storing:** Store in an airtight container in the fridge for up to 2 days.

# Pickled Mustard Seeds

### Makes 1¾ cup [390 g]

I originally tasted these mustard seeds on a cheese board at one of my favorite local eateries and soon realized I love them as a topping on pretty much everything. They add a burst of acidic flavor and are extra delicious with creamy soups because they bring in texture.

¼ cup [45 g] yellow mustard seeds

½ cup [120 ml] white wine vinegar

1 Tbsp sugar

½ tsp salt

**1.** Place the mustard seeds in a small saucepan and cover with cold water. Bring to a boil over high heat. Remove from the heat and drain through a fine-mesh strainer, discarding the water, and repeat this process two more times.

**2.** Return the seeds to the saucepan. Stir in the vinegar, sugar, salt, and ½ cup [120 ml] cold water and bring to a boil over high heat. Remove from the heat and transfer everything into a sealable jar. Refrigerate overnight so the flavors can develop, and serve the next day.

☞ **Storing:** Store for up to 1 month in an airtight container in the fridge.

# Green Romesco

### Makes 1 cup [240 g]

I developed this recipe for my Summer Garden Minestrone (page 181), but it's delicious swirled into so many soups; try the Pressure Cooker Black Bean Soup (page 135) or the Smoked Paprika Tortilla Soup (page 73).

1 green bell pepper, cut into 2 in [5 cm] pieces

1 poblano pepper, cut into 2 in [5 cm] pieces

1 jalapeño, cut into 2 in [5 cm] pieces

2 garlic cloves, crushed

3 Tbsp olive oil

¼ tsp salt

½ cup [60 g] slivered almonds

½ cup [20 g] chopped fresh cilantro

1 tsp red wine vinegar

⅛ tsp freshly ground black pepper

**1.** Preheat the oven to 400°F [200°C] and line a baking sheet with foil. Place the bell pepper, poblano, jalapeño, and garlic on the prepared baking sheet and toss with 1 Tbsp of the oil and the salt. Roast for 25 minutes, tossing halfway through, or until starting to brown in spots. When 8 minutes remain, add the almonds to the pan and roast for the remaining time.

**2.** Alternatively, heat an outdoor grill to medium. Add the bell pepper, poblano, jalapeño, and garlic into a grill basket and grill for 25 minutes, tossing often, or until starting to brown in spots. Toast the almonds in the oven on a baking sheet for 8 minutes.

**3.** Transfer the peppers and garlic to a high-speed blender along with the cilantro, vinegar, pepper, and ½ cup [120 ml] water. Blend on high speed until smooth, about 2 minutes. Taste and season with salt and pepper as needed.

☞ **Storing:** Let cool before storing in an airtight container in the fridge for up to 2 days.

## Citrus-Artichoke White Pesto

### Makes 1¼ cup [300 g]

This rich pesto swaps traditional basil for marinated artichoke hearts and ricotta, becoming a creamy sauce perfect for swirling into brothy soups that could use a touch of richness. I love buttery pecans here, but you could go traditional with pine nuts or swap in pistachios or walnuts.

¼ cup [30 g] toasted pecans

1 garlic clove, crushed

½ cup [120 g] ricotta

¼ cup [15 g] grated pecorino cheese

3 oz [90 g] jarred artichoke hearts, drained and finely chopped

1 tsp grated lemon zest

1 Tbsp fresh lemon juice

¼ tsp red pepper flakes

¼ tsp salt

⅛ tsp freshly ground black pepper

¼ cup [60 ml] olive oil

**1.** Add the pecans and garlic to a food processor fitted with the blade attachment and pulse five to seven times, or until they've broken down into small pieces. Add the ricotta, pecorino, artichoke hearts, lemon zest and juice, red pepper flakes, salt, and pepper. Turn on the food processor and slowly pour in the oil. Let it run until a chunky pesto has formed, 5 seconds more. Taste and season with salt, lemon juice, and red pepper flakes as needed.

☞ **Storing:** Store in an airtight container in the fridge for up to 3 days.

## Honeyed Feta with Black & White Sesame Seeds

### Makes 16 pieces

Rolling small triangles of feta in a honey mixture and then covering them in toasted sesame seeds makes a visually pleasing, sweet-and-salty topping for your creamy soups. These are especially tasty with Coconut Pumpkin Curry Red Lentil Stew (page 59) or the Carrot-Orange-Ginger Soup (page 85). If you can't find black sesame seeds (check where they keep sushi supplies in your grocery store or the spice section), then you can use all white; they won't be as visually striking but will still taste delicious.

8 oz [230 g] feta cheese (not crumbled)

3 Tbsp black sesame seeds

3 Tbsp white sesame seeds

1 Tbsp honey

**1.** Cut the block of feta into four equal squares. Cut those down the middle to create two thinner squares from each piece, for a total of eight pieces. Cut those squares diagonally to create 16 triangles.

**2.** In a small skillet over medium-low heat, toast the black and white sesame seeds, stirring often, until the white ones have started to take on a golden hue, about 3 minutes. Remove from the heat and transfer to a shallow dish or bowl.

**3.** Whisk the honey together with 1 Tbsp of warm water in a shallow bowl. Dip the feta into the thinned honey, being careful not to crumble it, and then roll in the sesame seeds, pressing the feta lightly into the seeds to help them stick. Repeat with all the feta triangles.

☞ **Storing:** Store leftovers in an airtight container in the fridge for up to 3 days.

# Fennel-Rye Croutons

**Makes 2 cups [80 g]**

These croutons add the perfect crunch to any of the creamy soups in this book (my favorite is the Broccoli-Cheddar Soup [page 111] or the Gruyère, Cauliflower & Potato Soup [page 31]) and are also great in salads (see page 132).

2 Tbsp olive oil

1 garlic clove, minced

½ tsp fennel seeds, chopped

¼ tsp salt

2 cups [60 g] rye bread, cut into 1 in [2.5 cm] pieces

**1.** Preheat the oven to 350°F [180°C]. In a large bowl, whisk together the oil, garlic, fennel seeds, and salt. Add the bread cubes and toss until completely coated with the oil mixture. Spread into an even layer on a baking sheet and toast for 10 minutes, tossing halfway through. Serve right away.

☞ **Storing:** If wanting to make in advance, skip adding the garlic and store these in an airtight container at room temperature for up to 2 days.

# Smoked Gouda Grilled Cheese Croutons

**Makes 16 large croutons**

These croutons may be simple, but they pack a ton of flavor! Make a batch when you whip up your Roasted Tomato Soup (page 37). They add texture while also gesturing to the comforting classic menu of grilled cheese and tomato soup.

4 slices white or sourdough bread

2 Tbsp unsalted butter, at room temperature

4 oz [115 g] smoked Gouda cheese, shredded

1 Tbsp Dijon mustard

1 Tbsp olive oil

**1.** Start by making two sandwiches. Spread ½ Tbsp of the butter onto each of the slices of bread. Flip the bread slices over so that the butter is facing down. Divide the cheese between two of the bread slices. Spread ½ Tbsp of mustard on each of the two remaining slices and place on top of the cheese-covered slices, mustard-side down, so that the cheese and mustard are on the inside of the sandwiches.

**2.** Heat the oil in a medium skillet over medium heat. Add the sandwiches, lower the heat to medium-low, cover, and cook until golden brown, about 3 minutes on each side. Remove from the heat and transfer to a cutting board. Cut each sandwich into 1 in [2.5 cm] squares and serve on top of soup.

☞ **Storing:** Smoked Gouda Grilled Cheese Croutons are best enjoyed the same day but can be stored in an airtight container in the fridge for up to 2 days.

# Candied Bacon

### Serves 6 as a topping

If you are looking to add a pop of flavor, the mix of sweet and savory makes this bacon an ideal topping for most soups. In order to achieve even cooking, you'll want to place the bacon on a wire rack (I use my cookie cooling rack), which allows air to circulate. I also wrap the baking sheet in foil for easy clean up and place that under the rack to catch the rendered bacon fat.

½ cup [100 g] packed brown sugar

2 Tbsp maple syrup

½ tsp freshly ground black pepper

12 oz [340 g] bacon

1. Preheat the oven to 325°F [170°C]. Line a baking sheet with foil and place a wire cooling rack on top.

2. In a small bowl, whisk together the sugar, maple syrup, and black pepper. Arrange the bacon in a single layer on the cooling rack.

3. Sprinkle half of the sugar mixture over the top of the bacon, and bake for 15 minutes. Flip the bacon and sprinkle the remaining sugar mixture on the other side of bacon. Bake until turning dark and crispy, 15 to 20 minutes more.

4. Remove from the oven and cool completely (the sugar will harden up as it cools, which helps it stick to the bacon). Enjoy as strips or transfer to a cutting board and chop into small pieces to sprinkle over soup.

☞ **Storing:** Store leftovers in an airtight container in the fridge for up to 2 days and reheat over low heat in a skillet.

# Spicy Shrimp

### Serves 4

Since we live in a landlocked area of the Midwest, Wyatt usually buys his shrimp frozen, but fresh would also work wonderfully if you have access to it (just skip thawing). He loves spicy food, so he finds that the touch of heat on the shrimp works wonderfully for soup toppers. If you aren't a fan of spicy food, feel free to use less chili powder and swap in cumin or sweet paprika to tame the heat.

1 Tbsp chili powder

1 tsp smoked paprika

½ tsp salt

¼ tsp freshly ground black pepper

1 lb [455 g] large, raw, peeled, and deveined shrimp, thawed if frozen

Olive oil or neutral oil, such as canola or vegetable oil, for frying

1. In a medium bowl, whisk together the chili powder, smoked paprika, salt, and pepper. Add the shrimp and toss to coat.

2. Add enough oil to a medium skillet to coat the bottom of it and warm it over medium heat. Line a plate with a paper towel. Working in batches, fry the shrimp until cooked all the way through and opaque, 2 minutes on each side. Transfer to the prepared plate and repeat with the rest of the shrimp. Serve immediately.

# Shredded Chicken

### Serves 4

We developed this recipe so that the chicken can be added in the last few minutes of simmering your soup to take on a bit of flavor from the broth. We kept the seasoning for this shredded chicken very minimal so it can be a blank canvas. Wyatt finds that the easiest way to shred the chicken is to use two forks to break the meat apart as soon as it is cool enough to touch.

1 lb [455 g] boneless, skinless chicken breasts (about 2)

Water or chicken broth, for poaching

½ tsp garlic powder (optional)

½ tsp salt

¼ tsp freshly ground black pepper

**1.** Place the chicken in a medium saucepan and add enough water or chicken broth to cover the chicken by 1 in [2.5 cm]. Add the garlic powder (if using), salt, and pepper and bring to a boil over high heat. Lower the heat to medium-low and simmer until the internal temperature of the chicken is at 165°F [75°C], 12 to 15 minutes. Remove the chicken from the pan and let cool slightly. While it's still warm, shred with two forks.

☞ **Storing:** Serve immediately, or cool to room temperature, then refrigerate in an airtight container for up to 3 days.

# Mini Meatballs

### Makes 28 meatballs / Serves 4

These mini meatballs don't take long; you can even bake them while your soup is simmering. Serve them on the side so people can decide if and how many meatballs they'd like in their soup. If you have leftovers, these meatballs are great in subs or on top of spaghetti as well!

½ cup [70 g] finely diced white onion

¼ cup [15 g] panko bread crumbs

¼ cup [8 g] finely grated Parmesan cheese

¼ cup [10 g] chopped fresh parsley

3 Tbsp whole-milk ricotta

1 egg, lightly beaten

1 Tbsp tomato paste

2 garlic cloves, minced

1 tsp salt

¼ tsp freshly ground black pepper

1 lb [455 g] lean ground beef

Olive oil, for brushing

**1.** Preheat the oven to 400°F [200°C] and grease a baking sheet.

**2.** In a large bowl, mix together the onion, bread crumbs, Parmesan, parsley, ricotta, egg, tomato paste, garlic, salt, and pepper. Using clean hands or a spatula, add the beef and mix just until combined.

**3.** Scoop 1 Tbsp of the meat mixture, roll between your hands to create a small ball, and place it on the prepared baking sheet. Repeat until you have about twenty-eight meatballs. Brush with olive oil and bake for 12 to 15 minutes, or until starting to brown and the internal temperature reaches 165°F [75°C]. Turn on the broiler for 1 to 2 minutes, or until the tops have browned up, making sure they don't burn.

☞ **Storing:** Serve immediately, or cool to room temperature and refrigerate in an airtight container for up to 3 days, or freeze for up to 2 months.

# ACCOMPANiMENTS

# Italian-ish Chopped Salad with Apricot-Oregano Dressing

**Serves 6 to 8**

### Dressing

¼ cup [75 g] apricot jam

2 Tbsp red wine vinegar

1 Tbsp dried oregano

1 tsp Dijon mustard

½ tsp red pepper flakes

½ tsp salt

½ cup [120 ml] olive oil

### Salad

1 medium head iceberg lettuce, or 1 large head romaine lettuce, rinsed, dried, and torn into bite-size pieces

½ head radicchio, cored and torn into bite-size pieces

One 15½ oz [445 g] can chickpeas, rinsed

1 pint [320 g] cherry tomatoes, halved

½ cup [70 g] thinly sliced red onion

5 oz [140 g] provolone cheese, cut into ½ in [13 mm] dice

5 oz [140 g] jarred pepperoncini (about 10 small)

4 oz [115 g] green olives, pitted

2 Tbsp chopped fresh chives

This salad is super versatile, and the flavor is simple enough to go with any soup in this book. Feel free to swap in other veggies (think jarred artichoke hearts, chopped celery, carrot pieces, etc.), cheeses (such as Cheddar, Manchego, or Gruyère), and soft herbs (parsley! cilantro! and so on). I've come to appreciate the crisp blank canvas that iceberg lettuce lends here, but you could use romaine if that is your go-to.

1. **Make the dressing:** In a small bowl, whisk together the jam, vinegar, oregano, mustard, red pepper flakes, and salt. Slowly pour in the oil while whisking to emulsify the dressing. Set aside.

2. **Make the salad:** In a large serving bowl, toss together the iceberg, radicchio, chickpeas, cherry tomatoes, onion, provolone, pepperoncini, olives, and chives. Drizzle half the dressing into the salad and toss to coat. Serve right away with the remaining dressing on the side so people can add more if they'd like.

☞ **Storing:** Store dressing in an airtight container in the fridge for up to 3 days.

# Kale Salad with Parsley-Lemon Vinaigrette

**Serves 10 to 12**

## Dressing

¼ cup [60 ml] apple cider vinegar

2 Tbsp fresh lemon juice

¼ cup [10 g] chopped fresh parsley

1 tsp garlic powder

¼ tsp salt

½ cup [120 ml] olive oil

½ cup [70 g] dried cherries

## Salad

2 bunches (14 oz [400 g]) dinosaur kale

½ cup [70 g] roasted pepitas

1 cup [140 g] shredded carrots

4 oz [115 g] goat cheese, crumbled

Inspired by my G.O.A.T. favorite salad from a now-closed local burrito place (where it was dubbed "Highway to Kale"), here's my addictive rendition. I recommend using dinosaur kale (also sometimes called Tuscan kale or Lacinato kale) here, as I find it to be easier to clean and perhaps even a bit milder than other widely available varieties. Make the dressing first so the dried cherries can plump in it while you prepare everything else. Also feel free to swap out the cherries with dried cranberries or golden raisins if that's what you have on hand. I recommend tossing the salad with only half the dressing and serving the rest on the side so guests can decide how much dressing they want to use.

1. **Make the dressing:** In a small bowl, whisk together the vinegar, lemon juice, parsley, garlic powder, and salt. Slowly pour in the oil while whisking until the dressing is emulsified. Add the dried cherries and set aside.

2. **Make the salad:** Tear the kale leaves off their stems and into bite-size pieces. Discard the stems and transfer the leaves to a large serving bowl. Add the pepitas and shredded carrots and toss to combine.

3. Scoop the cherries out of the dressing and into the salad. Drizzle half of the dressing over all and toss to coat everything. Dot the goat cheese over the salad, and serve with the remaining dressing on the side.

☞ **Storing:** This is best served right away, but leftover salad and dressing can be stored in separate airtight containers in the fridge overnight.

# Peach-Poblano Slaw

**Serves 6**

½ medium red cabbage, thinly sliced

3 carrots, peeled and cut into small matchsticks

2 fresh peaches, thinly sliced

2 small or 1 large poblano peppers, thinly sliced

1 green onion, thinly sliced

¼ cup [60 ml] rice vinegar or white distilled vinegar

2 Tbsp olive oil

1 Tbsp fresh lemon juice

1 Tbsp hot sauce (omit if you don't like spice)

½ Tbsp honey

½ tsp salt

Freshly ground black pepper

¼ cup [35 g] roasted sunflower seeds

This crunchy slaw is the perfect contrast to any of my summer soups. Try it with Corn & Roasted Poblano Chowder (page 189) or one of the gazpachos (pages 169 and 173). Make it with peaches when they are at their peak—it's also delish with apricots or cherries!

**1.** In a medium bowl, gently (being careful not to bruise the peach slices) toss together the cabbage, carrots, peaches, poblanos, and green onion.

**2.** In a small bowl, whisk together the vinegar, oil, lemon juice, hot sauce, honey, salt, and a dash of freshly ground black pepper. Drizzle the dressing over the cabbage mixture and toss until completely coated. Taste and season with salt and pepper as needed.

**3.** Cover and refrigerate for 30 minutes to let the flavors blend. When ready to serve, sprinkle with sunflower seeds and enjoy chilled.

☞ **Storing:** This salad is best enjoyed day of, but it can be stored in the fridge in an airtight container overnight.

# Citrus Salad with Rosemary Candied Walnuts & Radicchio

**Serves 4 to 6 as a side**

### Dressing

3 Tbsp red wine vinegar

2 Tbsp blood orange juice (from 1 small blood orange)

1 tsp finely chopped fresh rosemary, plus more for serving

½ tsp salt

¼ tsp freshly ground black pepper

3 Tbsp olive oil

1 small shallot, thinly sliced

¼ cup [35 g] dried cranberries

### Candied Walnuts

½ cup [60 g] chopped walnuts

1 Tbsp brown sugar

½ Tbsp unsalted butter

1 tsp finely chopped fresh rosemary

½ tsp salt

### Salad

3 oranges (ideally 1 blood orange, 1 navel, and 1 Cara Cara for a variety of color)

1 head radicchio, ends trimmed and leaves separated or cut into bite-size pieces

¼ cup [35 g] sliced and pitted green olives

I love sturdy and crunchy bitter greens like endive and radicchio. Their bitterness can be bracing on their own, but mixing them with sweet fruit, fatty nuts, and an acidic dressing creates a wonderfully balanced salad perfect for pairing with a rich soup such as Gruyère, Cauliflower & Potato Soup (page 31) or French Onion Soup (page 107). When making this salad, I always start with the dressing and use it as a quick-pickling liquid for the shallot and dried cranberries.

1. **Make the dressing:** In a large bowl, whisk together the vinegar, blood orange juice, rosemary, salt, and pepper. Slowly pour in the oil while whisking until emulsified. Stir in the shallot and dried cranberries and set aside for the flavors to meld.

2. **Make the candied walnuts:** Line a baking sheet with parchment paper. Add the walnuts, brown sugar, butter, rosemary, and salt to a small skillet and sauté over medium-low heat, stirring often, until the butter and sugar have melted and are sticking to the walnuts, about 5 minutes. Remove from the heat and spread the walnuts in a single layer on the prepared baking sheet. Set aside to cool and harden for at least 5 minutes.

3. **Make the salad:** Use a knife to peel the oranges by slicing around the edges to remove all the skin and pith (white parts). Turn the oranges on their sides and cut into ½ in [13 mm] wheels (you could also cut into segments if you'd prefer, or do a little of both).

4. Toss the radicchio in the dressing and arrange the leaves on a serving platter. Scatter over the olives, oranges, walnuts, shallots, and cranberries, and drizzle any remaining dressing over the radicchio. Serve right away.

Serves 4

### Dressing

¼ cup [60 ml] apple cider vinegar

1 small shallot, thinly sliced

1 Tbsp Dijon mustard

2 tsp honey

½ tsp salt

¼ tsp freshly ground black pepper

⅓ cup [80 ml] olive oil

⅓ cup [45 g] dried cranberries

### Salad

2 lb [910 g] Brussels sprouts

½ cup [70 g] unsalted raw cashews

2 Tbsp brown sugar

½ Tbsp unsalted butter

1 Tbsp olive oil

¼ tsp salt

¼ cup [35 g] roasted sunflower seeds

# Brussels Sprouts Salad with Apple Cider Vinaigrette

Is it a salad or a slaw? Maybe a bit of both, and why not? By roasting some of the Brussels sprout leaves, you end up with crispy leaf chips that are a delicious contrast to raw shredded sprouts. I use cheese *a lot* in this book, so I left it out here because the salad was delicious without. But I doubt anyone would complain if you wanted to toss in a handful of crumbled feta or cubed provolone.

**1.** **Make the dressing:** In a large bowl, whisk together the vinegar, shallot, mustard, honey, ½ tsp of the salt, and the pepper. Slowly pour in ⅓ cup [80 ml] of the oil while whisking until emulsified. Stir in the dried cranberries and set aside for the flavors to meld.

**2.** **Make the salad:** Preheat the oven to 375°F [190°C] and line two baking sheets with parchment paper. Trim the ends of the sprouts, pull off the largest outer leaves, and set them aside in a medium bowl (you should end up with about 2½ cups [70 g] of sprout leaves). Thinly slice and then shred the rest of the sprouts (or use a food processor to shred) and transfer to the bowl with dressing. Toss until the sprouts are completely coated and set aside.

**3.** In a small skillet, combine the cashews, brown sugar, butter, and a pinch of salt and sauté over medium-low heat, stirring often, until the butter and sugar have melted and are sticking to the cashews, about 5 minutes. Remove from the heat and spread the cashews in a single layer on one of the prepared baking sheets. Set aside to cool and harden for at least 5 minutes.

**4.** Toss the Brussels sprout leaves with the oil and salt and spread in a single layer on the other baking sheet. Roast for 7 minutes, stirring halfway through, until starting to brown.

**5.** Transfer the raw sprouts along with the dressing to a serving platter and top with the sunflower seeds, candied cashews, and the crispy Brussels sprout leaves. Serve right away.

# Winter Farro Salad with Agrodolce Sauce

**Serves 6 to 8**

### Salad

1 large sweet potato, cut into ½ in [13 mm] cubes (about 4 cups [560 g])

¼ cup [60 ml] olive oil

1 Tbsp plus ¾ tsp salt

1½ cups [270 g] farro, rinsed

### Dressing

1 cup [240 ml] white wine vinegar, champagne vinegar, or rice vinegar

½ cup [100 g] sugar

1 small shallot, thinly sliced

3 garlic cloves, thinly sliced

2 tsp red pepper flakes

1 cup [100 g] chopped radicchio

¼ cup [10 g] chopped fresh parsley

4 oz [115 g] feta cheese, crumbled

¼ tsp freshly ground black pepper

I yelped with excitement when I took a bite of this salad for the first time—it's that good. The sweet heat from the agrodolce sauce plays beautifully with the salty feta and bitter radicchio. For anyone not familiar, agrodolce is an Italian condiment made by reducing vinegar and sugar. I've pumped up the flavor even more here with a hit of garlic and red pepper flakes to turn it into the perfect dressing for this grain salad.

Grain salads are delicious fresh but oftentimes even tastier once they've had a few hours to sit and develop flavor. So I like to make this grain salad the night before I am planning to enjoy it.

**1.** **Make the salad:** Preheat the oven to 400°F [200°C] and line a baking sheet with parchment paper. Add the sweet potato to the prepared baking sheet and toss with 1 Tbsp of the oil and ¼ tsp of the salt. Spread into an even layer and roast for 20 to 22 minutes, or until tender. Set aside to cool.

**2.** Meanwhile, bring 8 cups [2 L] of water to a boil in a large saucepan. Stir in the farro and 1 Tbsp of the salt and simmer over medium-low heat until the farro is tender with a slight chew, 15 to 30 minutes. Drain and transfer to the baking sheet with the sweet potatoes. Spread it out on the sheet and cool for at least 15 minutes.

**3.** **Make the dressing:** In a small nonreactive saucepan, combine the vinegar and sugar and bring to a simmer over medium heat. Simmer, stirring every so often to dissolve the sugar, until the mixture is syrupy and reduced by half, 10 to 12 minutes. Remove from the heat and stir in the shallot, garlic, and red pepper flakes.

**4.** Transfer the farro and sweet potatoes to a large serving bowl. Add the radicchio, parsley, feta, the remaining ½ tsp of salt, and black pepper and stir to combine. Drizzle the dressing, along with all the red pepper flakes, garlic, and shallots we added to it, into the salad and toss to combine. Taste and season with salt and pepper as needed.

☞ **Storing:** The salad can be enjoyed right away but the flavors develop a bit more if you cover and refrigerate for a few hours until ready to serve.

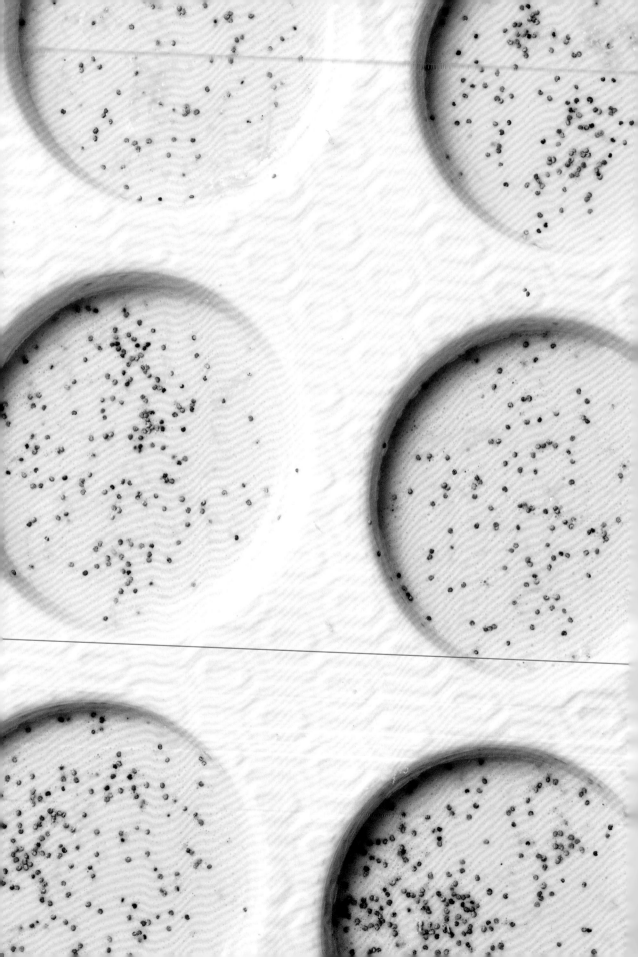

# Lemon-Poppyseed Popovers

**Makes 12 popovers**

4 eggs, warmed in a cup of hot water for 10 minutes

1½ cups [360 ml] whole milk, at room temperature

½ tsp salt

½ tsp sugar

1½ cups [210 g] all-purpose flour

3 Tbsp unsalted butter, melted

1½ Tbsp poppyseeds

1 Tbsp grated lemon zest (from 2 large lemons)

It's important these go into a very hot oven, so wait to make the batter until your oven is preheated. Avoid opening the oven door while these bake to keep them from collapsing. These aren't sweet, making them perfect for serving alongside soup with a little butter or even as a vehicle for dipping.

**1.** Preheat the oven to 450°F [230°C] and grease a twelve-cup metal muffin pan.

**2.** To the carafe of a blender, add, in this order, the eggs, milk, salt, sugar, and flour and blend until completely combined and light and frothy. Add the butter, poppyseeds, and lemon zest and use a whisk to hand whisk into the batter until combined.

**3.** Pour the batter into the muffin pan, filling each cup three-quarters full. Bake for 20 minutes, then turn the oven down to 350°F [180°C] and bake for 10 minutes or until golden brown.

☞ **Storing:** These are best enjoyed same day, but you could make the batter up to a day ahead and store in the fridge if wanting to do some make-ahead prep.

# Quick Yogurt Flatbread

**Makes 8 flatbreads**

2 cups [280 g] all-purpose flour, plus more for rolling

½ Tbsp baking powder

1 tsp salt

1½ cups [360 g] plain Greek yogurt

4 Tbsp [55 g] ghee, unsalted butter, or olive oil

Chopped fresh parsley or minced garlic, for serving (optional)

This is my go-to when I want to serve homemade bread with my soups but I'm short on time. Top with chopped parsley or minced garlic to jazz them up. You can grill these (just brush the bread with oil instead of melting it in the pan) if making in the warmer months.

1. In a medium bowl, whisk together the flour, baking powder, and salt. Make a well in the center of the dry ingredients and add the yogurt. Stir to create a shaggy dough.

2. Transfer the dough to a floured surface and knead until smooth, 2 to 3 minutes. If the dough is sticking to the counter, add more flour, 1 Tbsp at a time, until it no longer sticks but remains very wet. Cover loosely with plastic wrap and set aside to rest for 15 minutes.

3. Divide the dough half and then each half into quarters so you end up with eight even pieces. Working with one piece at a time, roll it out onto a heavily floured surface into an 8 in [20 cm] circle. After rolling, cover each piece with the plastic wrap to keep it from drying out.

4. In a medium (at least 10 in [25 cm]) skillet over medium heat, warm ½ Tbsp of the ghee. Add one piece of flatbread to the skillet and cook for 2 to 3 minutes on each side, or until cooked all the way through. Brush with more melted ghee and sprinkle with parsley or garlic, if desired. Transfer to a plate and repeat with the remaining flatbreads, adding ½ Tbsp ghee to the pan before cooking each.

☞ **Storing:** Store leftovers in an airtight container in the fridge for up to 2 days.

# Sun-Dried Tomato & Manchego Biscuits

**Makes 6 biscuits**

2 cups [280 g] all-purpose flour

1 Tbsp baking powder

1 tsp sugar

1 tsp salt

4 Tbsp [55 g] unsalted butter (3 Tbsp very cold and 1 Tbsp melted)

2 oz [55 g] Manchego cheese, cut into ¼ in [6 mm] cubes

2 Tbsp chopped oil-packed sun-dried tomatoes

¾ cup [180 ml] buttermilk

I've made a lot of so-so biscuits in my life. So when I nailed this crispy-on-the-outside, tender-on-the-inside version, I knew I'd never deviate from this formula. Feel free to get creative with other mix-ins: Cubed cooked sweet potato, goat cheese, or chives and blue cheese chunks would be delicious swaps.

1. Preheat the oven to 375°F [190°C] and line a baking sheet with parchment paper.

2. In a medium bowl, whisk together the flour, baking powder, sugar, and salt. Cut 3 Tbsp of very cold butter into small cubes and add to the dry ingredients. Use clean hands or a pastry cutter to work the butter into the dry ingredients until only pea-size pieces of butter remain. Stir in the cheese and tomatoes.

3. Drizzle in the buttermilk and use your clean hands to work it into the dry ingredients until a shaggy dough forms. Transfer the dough to a floured surface and pat, being careful not to overwork the dough, into a 6 by 4 in [15 by 10 cm] rectangle about 1 in [2.5 cm] thick. Cut out six biscuits by cutting down the rectangle lengthwise and then cutting those two strips into three even rectangles each.

4. Evenly space the biscuits on the prepared baking sheet and brush with the 1 Tbsp of melted butter. Bake for 15 to 20 minutes or until browned on top.

☞ **Storing:** Store leftover biscuits in an airtight container in the fridge for up to 2 days (if you are not adding cheese to your dough, then you can store these at room temperature for 2 days).

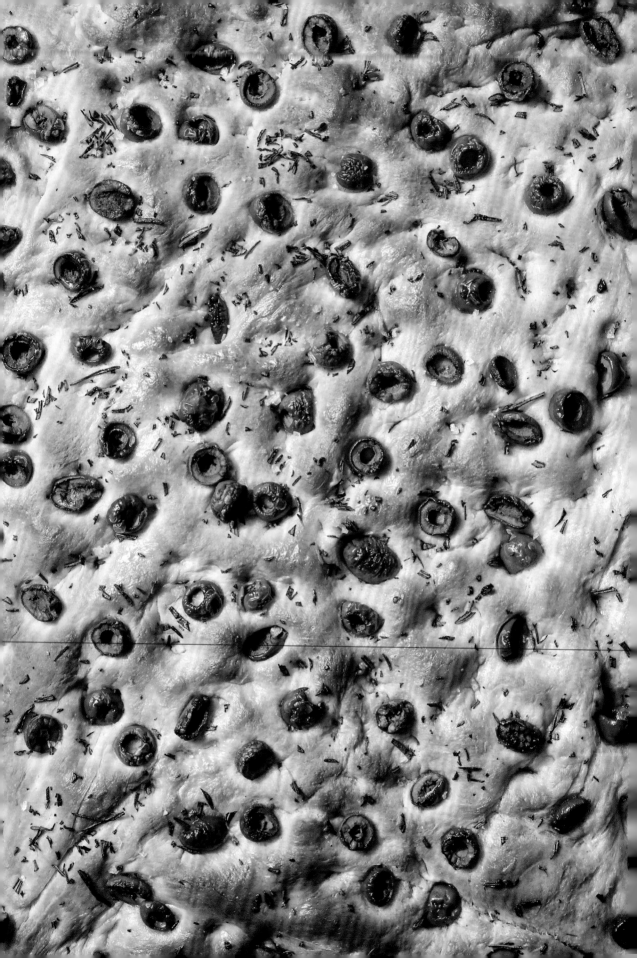

## Serves 16

2 cups [480 ml] warm water
(110°F [45°C])

2½ tsp active dry yeast

2 tsp sugar

5 cups [700 g] all-purpose flour

1 Tbsp fine sea salt

1 cup [240 ml] olive oil, plus more
for the bowl

2 Tbsp chopped fresh rosemary

5 oz [140 g] jar green olives
(about 36 olives), halved

Flaky sea salt, for serving
(optional)

# Green Olive & Rosemary Focaccia

Focaccia is my go-to bread for when I'm hosting. It yields a big sheet pan's worth of carb and always comes out tender and soft. I know 1 cup [240 ml] of olive oil is going to sound like a lot, but the oil is what gives this bread its crispy exterior and pillowy interior.

**1.** Combine ¼ cup [60 ml] of the warm water, the yeast, and sugar in a small bowl and let sit for 10 minutes, or until bubbly.

**2.** In the bowl of a stand mixer fitted with the dough attachment, add the flour and fine sea salt and mix for a few seconds to combine. Add ½ cup [120 ml] of the oil, the yeast mixture, and the remaining 1¾ cup [420 ml] of warm water and knead on medium speed until the dough comes together, about 30 seconds. Increase the speed to medium-high and knead for 5 minutes, until the dough is soft and elastic. Remove the dough, coat the bowl with olive oil, and transfer the dough back into the oiled bowl. Cover with a clean dish towel and place in a warm location for 1 hour, or until doubled in size.

**3.** Drizzle the remaining ½ cup [120 ml] of oil into a half sheet pan (18 by 13 in [46 by 33 cm]). With clean hands, press the dough into the prepared pan. Turn the dough over to coat the other side with oil and continue to press the dough into the pan with your fingertips, making sure the dough stretches as much as possible across the pan (it's OK if the dough springs back a bit and doesn't stay all the way in the corners). Cover and place in a warm spot until doubled in size, about 1 hour.

**4.** Preheat the oven to 425°F [220°C]. Uncover the dough and use clean hands to press the dough all over, leaving indents over the dough, and pushing it into the corners if it sprang back previously. Scatter it with the rosemary and lightly press the olives into the dough.

**5.** Bake for 20 to 25 minutes, or until the focaccia has browned on the top. Remove from the oven and sprinkle with a few pinches of flaky sea salt, if desired. Serve warm.

☞ **Storing:** Store wrapped in plastic at room temperature for up to 2 days.

# Cheddar & Pickled Jalapeño Dutch Oven Bread

**Makes 1 loaf**

1¾ cups [420 ml] warm water (110°F [45°C])

2½ tsp active dry yeast

1 tsp sugar

4 cups [560 g] bread flour

¼ cup [60 ml] plus 1 tsp olive oil, plus more for the bowl

1 tsp salt

4 oz [115 g] Cheddar cheese, shredded

1 oz [30 g] Parmesan cheese, grated

¼ cup [60 g] chopped pickled jalapeño

If I could eat only one kind of bread for the rest of my life, it would be this loaf. It's packed full of cheese and jalapeños, and the texture is a perfect mix of a soft interior and a crunchy exterior. If you like a lot of spice, you might use fresh, seeded jalapeño pieces instead of pickled.

**1.** Combine ¼ cup [60 ml] of the warm water, the yeast, and sugar in a small bowl and let sit for 10 minutes, or until bubbly.

**2.** In the bowl of a stand mixer fitted with a bread hook, add the flour, ¼ cup [60 ml] of the oil, the salt, yeast mixture, and the remaining 1½ cups [360 ml] of warm water. Mix on low until combined, then turn to medium-high speed and mix for 3 minutes or until a soft and sticky dough forms. Set aside 2 Tbsp of the Cheddar and add the rest to the bowl along with the Parmesan and pickled jalapeño. Mix on medium until the mix-ins are completely incorporated.

**3.** Remove the dough from the bowl, grease the bowl with oil, and then transfer the dough back into the bowl. Cover with a clean towel and let rise until doubled in bulk, about 2 hours.

**4.** Uncover, punch the dough down, and re-cover and let rise for another hour. After 30 minutes, preheat the oven to 450°F [230°C] and place a large Dutch oven in the oven to heat.

**5.** When the second rise is done, transfer the dough onto a sheet of parchment paper and, if needed, gently reshape into a ball. Brush the top with the remaining 1 tsp of oil and sprinkle with the reserved 2 Tbsp of Cheddar.

**6.** Using oven mitts, carefully remove the hot pot from the oven. Pick up the dough by the corners of the parchment paper and carefully transfer it to the pot along with the parchment paper. Cover and bake for 30 minutes, remove the lid, and bake for another 20 minutes, or until the internal temperature of the bread reaches 190°F [90°C].

**7.** Transfer to a wire rack and cool completely before slicing.

☞ **Storing:** Store leftovers in an airtight container in the fridge for up to 3 days.

**Makes 1 loaf**

5 Tbsp [70 g] unsalted butter

1 cup [140 g] yellow cornmeal

1 cup [140 g] all-purpose flour

¼ cup [50 g] brown sugar

1 Tbsp baking powder

¾ tsp salt

½ tsp baking soda

½ tsp ground cinnamon

¼ tsp ground ginger

⅛ tsp grated nutmeg

One 15 oz [430 g] can pumpkin purée

½ cup [120 g] sour cream

2 eggs

⅓ cup [45 g] raw pepitas

# Brown Butter Pumpkin Cornbread

We are steering pretty far from traditional cornbread with this recipe, but the flavors here are subtle enough to complement most soups while being unique enough to keep it interesting. The pepita topping gives your cornbread an extra crunch, while the sour cream helps keeps it on the softer side. This bread is delicious warm with just a pat of butter and perfect for dunking into chilis (try it with Chipotle Cocoa Three-Bean Chili, page 117) or stews (such as Caramelized Cabbage Barley Stew, page 65).

1. Preheat the oven to 400°F [200°C] and grease a 9 in [23 cm] round cake pan.

2. In a small saucepan or skillet over medium heat, melt 4 Tbsp [55 g] of the butter. Swirl the butter around the pan slightly, watching it closely, and after about 2 minutes, it should start to bubble. Let it bubble for 1 or 2 minutes or until you start to see small flecks of brown form on the bottom of the pan. Remove from the heat and set aside to cool.

3. In a large bowl, whisk together the cornmeal, flour, brown sugar, baking powder, salt, baking soda, cinnamon, ginger, and nutmeg until well combined. Make a well in the center of the dry ingredients and add the pumpkin, sour cream, eggs, and cooled brown butter. Whisk the wet ingredients together until combined (it's OK if some of the dry ingredients get in) and then fold the dry ingredients into the wet just until everything is combined. Mix only until there are no more dry parts; do not overmix.

4. Transfer the batter to the prepared cake pan and smooth the top so that it's even. Sprinkle the pepitas over the top and gently press them into the batter. Melt the remaining 1 Tbsp of butter in the microwave and drizzle over the top.

5. Cover with foil and bake for 20 minutes. Uncover and bake for an additional 5 to 10 minutes, or until a toothpick inserted in the center comes out clean.

☞ **Storing:** Wrap leftover Brown Butter Pumpkin Cornbread in foil and store at room temperature for 2 days.

**Makes 1 loaf**

3 cups [420 g] all-purpose flour

2 Tbsp sugar

1 Tbsp baking powder

½ tsp salt

12 oz [360 ml] light beer,
such as Corona or Miller Lite

½ cup [70 g] dried cranberries

2 chipotles in adobo sauce,
chopped, plus 1 Tbsp
adobo sauce

4 Tbsp [55 g] unsalted butter,
melted

# Cranberry Chili Beer Bread

This is a dense bread, perfect for chilly nights when you are craving something hearty. This bread is so easy to make that I always turn to it when I'm feeling too exhausted from the day to put too much effort into dinner. Just make sure you don't overwork the dough, or it will end up tough.

**1.** Preheat the oven to 375°F [190°C] and grease a loaf pan.

**2.** In a medium bowl, whisk together the flour, sugar, baking powder, and salt. Make a well in the center of the dry ingredients and pour in the beer. Fold the dry ingredients into the wet just until there are no dry spots remaining, being careful not to overmix. Fold in the cranberries, chipotles, and adobo sauce and transfer the dough to the prepared loaf pan.

**3.** Smooth the top of the dough in the loaf pan and pour the melted butter over it. Bake for 1 hour, or until the top is crispy and the internal temperature is 190°F [90°C].

☞ **Storing:** Store leftover bread in an airtight container at room temperature for up to 3 days.

Thank you so much to Wyatt, my collaborator and husband, for always putting on a smile when getting roped into my projects and for letting me get our kitchen dirty over and over again for months on end.

Thank you to my agent, Cindy Uh, for always being the best advocate and going above and beyond throughout all the years we've worked together. None of this would be possible without your persistence, negotiation skills, and constant support! I'm forever grateful for the time you've spent working on projects with me.

Thank you so much to everyone at Chronicle Books, particularly Sarah Billingsley, Claire Gilhuly, Lizzie Vaughan, Jessica Ling, Tera Killip, Steve Kim, Samantha Simon, and Keely Thomas-Menter for all the hard work that went into bringing this book to life. And thank you to all the wonderful people working on the distribution and retail side to help get this book into readers' hands.

Thank you so much to all of the recipe testers, friends, and family who took time to make sure these recipes would be a success in any type of kitchen: Alex Smith, Barbara Brosher, Ella Hartley, Erica Sagon, Jan Davis, Kacy Skelly, Kaleen Fry, Leslie Noggle, Megan MacDonald, Irasema, Renne Payne, Roy Kappel, Ryan Boyce, Shaina Dwiel, Stephanie Blandford, and Susie Tanney.

A big thank you to Leah Lukas, Jason Lukas, my mom, and Wyatt (again!) for assisting during photoshoot days. Those are always some of the most exciting, stressful, exhausting, and rewarding days of the process and wouldn't be nearly as fun and productive without your help.

And finally, thanks so much to you for picking up, reading, and cooking through this cookbook. ♥

# Index

## M

## N

## O

## P